## 2022-2023

# Prayer Journal

**This journal belongs to:**

_____

© 2022 Novalis Publishing Inc.

Cover: Jamie Wyatt
Interior design and layout: Jessica Llewellyn

Published in Canada by Novalis

Publishing Office
1 Eglinton Ave East, Suite 800
Toronto, Ontario, Canada
M4P 3A1

Head Office
4475 Frontenac Street
Montréal, Québec, Canada
H2H 2S2

www.novalis.ca

ISBN (for Canada):
978-2-89830-110-0

Published in the United States by Bayard, Inc.

One Montauk Avenue, Suite 200
New London, CT 06320

www.livingwithchrist.us

ISBN (for USA):
978-1-62785-715-4

Cataloguing in Publication is available from Library and Archives Canada.

Printed in Canada.

We acknowledge the support of the Government of Canada.

5    4    3    2    1      19    18    17    16    15

*Prayer is the best weapon we possess.*
*It is the key that opens the heart of God.*

—*St. Thomas Aquinas*

# *Why journal?*

SPIRITUAL JOURNALING IS a form of prayer. Far beyond recapping our life's events, the exercise of journaling helps us to express our spiritual life. Our written words capture our spiritual experiences, thoughts, struggles, victories – and essentially form a prayer through which we communicate to God what lies in our innermost self.

The exercise of spiritual journaling does not require us to be experienced in such a practice, nor are there any specific guidelines. When we journal, we need not worry about style or formalities. Just as in our regular prayers, Jesus wishes us to speak freely, simply, and honestly what is in our heart.

This journal provides a guideline to your prayer exercise in the **Responding to the Word** section each day, where you will find a question that is directly connected to the readings of the day. If this question is helpful, feel free to use it, but do not feel constrained by it.

Spiritual journaling will essentially enlarge our vision and lead to a greater understanding of our spiritual journey.

# *Prayer for the Help of the Holy Spirit*

Come, Holy Spirit,
fill the hearts of your faithful
and kindle in them the fire of your love.
Send forth your Spirit
and they shall be created,
and you shall renew the face of the earth.
O God, who by the light of the Holy Spirit,
did instruct the hearts of the faithful,
grant that by the same Holy Spirit
we may be truly wise
and ever enjoy his consolations.
Through the same Christ Our Lord.
Amen.

# 1st Sunday of Advent

DURING ADVENT, WE prepare for Christmas. Christmas is our encounter with God – or, more precisely, the coming of the Lord into the world so that *we* might encounter *him* – and Advent is the time during which we get ready for this encounter. But what is the "coming of the Lord"?

In today's first reading and the psalm, the way to encounter God is to go to a particular place – specifically the Temple in Jerusalem. Here, we may be instructed in living according to the ways of God. In the Gospel, Jesus speaks of the Day of Judgment: a future, though not-too-distant, coming of the Lord. Jesus warns us to be ready for that day, but does not tell us how to prepare.

In the second reading, St. Paul gives us some idea of how we might get ready: by living honorably; by putting on the Lord Jesus Christ. This can only mean that we live not only according to what Jesus teaches, but also to *how* Jesus lives: without sin; prayerfully; prophetically; and in giving of ourselves lovingly to others, even our enemies, without limit.

In doing so, we will find that the "coming of the Lord" is a reality not only outside us, but also *within* each of us. Indeed, the Lord comes to each of us, into the very fabric of our being, again today in our celebration of the Eucharist.

*Rev. Armand Mercier*

## People and Prayers to Remember this Week

_____

_____

_____

*Readings of the Day* ─────────────────────────

Isaiah 2.1-5                     Romans 13.11-14
Psalm 122                        Matthew 24.37-44

**Responding to the Word**

**Jesus reminds us that God often comes suddenly into the ordinary events of our lives. What must I do to be better prepared to encounter God?**

_____

_____

_____

_____

_____

_____

_____

_____

## Final Thoughts …

## Feasts this Week

**November 30  St Andrew**
**December 3    St Francis Xavier**

# 2nd Sunday of Advent

TODAY WE MEET John the Baptist in the wilderness. Matthew's gospel introduces him without any explanation because no introduction was needed. He was a great figure in the Jewish world of his day, not only in Judea but right across the Mediterranean. In the Acts of the Apostles (19.1-7), Paul comes across a group of John's disciples in Ephesus in what today is Turkey.

In one way, John was a deeply traditional figure in Judaism; in another way, he was a radical, new figure. He dressed like the prophet Elijah and went out, like Elijah, into the wilderness, calling people back to the word of God. In several places in the gospels, people in fact compare him with Elijah. In another way, he was very new because he called people to repent of their sins and be baptized as a sign of their repentance. The popularity of his challenging message, which drew great crowds out into the desert for baptism, shows that the time was ripe for the message of Jesus.

Jesus completed what John began: he offered a baptism in the Holy Spirit for the forgiveness of sins and the start of a new age of peace. In a sinful and dangerous world, we yearn for that gift of the Spirit promised by Isaiah in today's first reading, proclaimed by John in his ministry, and brought to fulfillment by Jesus.

*Jennifer Cooper*

**People and Prayers to Remember this Week**

_____

_____

_____

*Readings of the Day* ————————————————

Isaiah 11.1-10                    Romans 15.4-9
Psalm 72                         Matthew 3.1-12

**Responding to the Word**

**The spirit-filled messiah will bring about greater justice
and peace. How is the Holy Spirit drawing me to create
better relationships in my life now?**

_____

_____

_____

_____

_____

_____

_____

_____

_____

_____

_____

_____

_____

_____

_____

_____

_____

_____

_____

_____

## Final Thoughts ...

_____

_____

_____

_____

## Feasts this Week

| | |
|---|---|
| **December 6** | **St Nicholas** |
| **December 7** | **St Ambrose** |
| **December 8** | **The Immaculate Conception<br>of the Blessed Virgin Mary** |
| **December 9** | **St Juan Diego Cuauhtlatoatzin** |
| **December 10** | **Our Lady of Loreto** |

# *Immaculate Conception of the Blessed Virgin Mary*

"FOR NOTHING WILL be impossible with God." From the beginning of our creation story, we struggle to believe that God can make right what we perceive to have gone wrong. Adam and Eve hide in the garden, and throughout salvation history, we are tempted to despair and disbelief.

The second reading makes clear that nothing can get in the way of God's loving pursuit of us. He was not thrown off by human sin, discouraged by our imperfection, or distanced from our fault; rather, "he chose us in Christ before the foundation of the world to be holy and blameless before him in love." We were made to belong to God's family, an adoption of radical love that casts out shame. So often, in the midst of our own challenges we buy into the lie that, even though God might work miracles out there somewhere, our brokenness or sin is just too big for God.

Where we might be tempted to see what could go wrong, Gabriel invites Mary to see – through Elizabeth's joy – the hopeful possibility that this almighty God will find a way through all obstacles to possibility. She believes the promise that nothing will be impossible. May we believe likewise and let God work miracles in our impossible places.

*Leah Perrault*

**People and Prayers to Remember this Week**

_____

_____

_____

*Readings of the Day* ──────────────────

Genesis 3.9-15, 20        Ephesians 1.3-6, 11-12

Psalm 98        Luke 1.26-38

**Responding to the Word**

**The angel tells Mary that nothing is impossible with God. When has God made the impossible possible in my life?**

_____

_____

_____

_____

_____

_____

_____

_____

_____

_____

## Final Thoughts …

# 3rd Sunday of Advent

WHAT A DIFFERENCE between last Sunday's gospel and this Sunday's! Last week, it was a confident, assertive John the Baptist who exploded onto the scene preaching repentance, judgment, and the coming Messiah. Today, we see a much different John. Imprisoned and disheartened, John questions whether Jesus is actually the One whose coming he had foretold.

But who can blame him? After all, the Messiah whose coming John had promised was to chop down the unworthy and burn the "chaff." Instead, Jesus was healing the lame and cleansing the leper. He certainly wasn't the kind of Messiah John had expected.

And what about our own expectations? If we are honest with ourselves, there may be times when Jesus doesn't fit into the nice, neat mold we have for him. Times, perhaps, when a prayer isn't answered the way we would like, or our idea about what is right and fair doesn't fit with gospel values. Then what do we do?

As the beginning of the new church year, Advent invites us to start over, to leave behind the familiar and venture into the unknown. Part of that can be letting go of pre-conceived notions about who Jesus is and how he should work in our lives, and opening ourselves up to new possibilities. With John the Baptist as our guide, let us begin today to discover anew the Jesus born into our world at Christmas.

*Teresa Whalen Lux*

**People and Prayers to Remember this Week**

*Readings of the Day*

Isaiah 35.1-6a, 10
Psalm 146

James 5.7-10
Matthew 11.2-11

**Responding to the Word**

Isaiah encourages us to be strong and fear not when God comes. What weakness and fear block my acceptance of God into my life?

_____

_____

_____

_____

_____

_____

_____

_____

_____

_____

_____

_____

_____

_____

## Final Thoughts ...

_____

_____

_____

_____

## Feasts this Week

**December 12   Our Lady of Guadalupe**
**December 13   St Lucy**
**December 14   St John of the Cross**

# 4th Sunday of Advent

ON THE FIRST Sunday of Advent, St. Paul told us "it is now the moment for you to wake from sleep," and we heard Jesus say to "keep awake." From the beginning of Advent we are reminded to be open to the Lord's presence and future coming. In today's gospel Joseph wakes from sleep literally and spiritually. "When Joseph awoke from sleep, he did as the Angel of the Lord commanded him."

Joseph no doubt felt confused, hurt, betrayed: the woman he was to marry was pregnant and he was not the father. Perhaps, like King Ahaz in the first reading, he was reluctant to ask God for guidance, for a sign. But Ahaz is given a sign and hope for the future in the promise of a child. For Christians, this is the deeper, more far-reaching promise of the Messiah – the Promised One. This promise will be fulfilled in Joseph's time: the young woman – a virgin – is with child.

Joseph, too, receives a sign, in his case in a dream. Now he is awake, for he has also been given discernment. He knows God's will and he will follow it. How can we awaken to God's presence and God's will? What signs does God send? Through Scripture, prayer, the Mass, the sacraments, other people – in these and other ways God wakes us from sleep to know and do his will.

*Dinah Simmons*

**People and Prayers to Remember this Week**

_____

_____

_____

*Readings of the Day* —————————————————————

Isaiah 7.10-14
Psalm 24

Romans 1.1-7
Matthew 1.18-24

**Responding to the Word**

**God offers to give Ahaz a sign of God's care for the people. What signs of God's care have I noticed recently?**

_____

_____

_____

_____

_____

_____

_____

_____

_____

_____

_____

_____

_____

_____

_____

_____

_____

_____

_____

_____

_____

_____

_____

_____

## Final Thoughts ...

_____

_____

_____

_____

## Feasts this Week

**December 21   St Peter Canisius**
**December 23   St John of Kanty**

# Nativity of the Lord (Christmas)

CHRISTMAS REMINDS US that God's promised presence took a totally unexpected turn with Jesus. Throughout the Bible, the question of where God may be found is of vital importance. The promise of God's presence sustained the Israelites through good times and bad. God kept that promise, but not always where or how they expected.

The birth of Jesus means God's presence, long acknowledged to be in the Temple's Holy of Holies, can now be found surprisingly in the lowly manger, in the tiny, vulnerable Christ child. This is the essence of the good news of great joy that the angels announce to the shepherds. This fulfillment of the promise of God's presence was totally unexpected by all.

No one thought that God would become enfleshed in a human being, especially one so insignificant by society's standards.

So where should we look for God today? Where is the lowly manger that reveals his saving presence? As always, God chooses to surprise us by lurking right under our noses, hiding in the weakest and most vulnerable among us – the "least of my brothers and sisters" who are hungry, thirsty, strangers, naked, sick, and imprisoned (Mt 25) – especially in our own families, neighbors, and co-workers. Like the shepherds, we must go there to find again our hidden Savior who "became flesh and made his dwelling among us" (Jn 1.14).

*Steve Mueller*

**People and Prayers to Remember this Week**

*Readings of the Day*

| *Mass during the Night:* | *Mass at Dawn:* | *Mass during the Day:* |
|---|---|---|
| Isaiah 9.2-4, 6-7 | Isaiah 62.11-12 | Isaiah 52.7-10 |
| Psalm 96 | Psalm 97 | Psalm 98 |
| Titus 2.11-14 | Titus 3.4-7 | Hebrews 1.1-6 |
| Luke 2.1-16 | Luke 2.15-20 | John 1.1-18 |

**Responding to the Word**

**Jesus is the human image of God. What particular aspect of God has Jesus revealed to me during this Advent?**

_____

_____

_____

_____

_____

_____

_____

_____

_____

_____

_____

_____

## Final Thoughts ...

_____

_____

_____

_____

## Feasts this Week

**December 26  St Stephen**
**December 27  St John**
**December 28  The Holy Innocents**
**December 29  St Thomas Becket**
**December 30  The Holy Family of Jesus, Mary, and Joseph**
**December 31  St Sylvester I**

# *Mary, the Holy Mother of God*

"HAIL MARY, FULL of grace," begins the prayer many of us have said thousands of times. While walking to work on dark January mornings in the Yukon, when the temperature hits 30 below, I find the repetition of these words helps me to focus and prepare for my day.

"Blessed art thou among women" singles out Mary, acknowledging the extraordinary role she agrees to assume. Through her, ancient hopes are fulfilled and the blessings and peace the Lord promises to Moses in the first reading are extended to all of us.

"Blessed is the fruit of thy womb, Jesus," affirms Mary as the Mother of God. As St. Paul states in the second reading, through this divine intervention in human history God sends the spirit of Jesus into our hearts, crying, "Abba! Father!" We are offered redemption from what enslaves us and the way is opened for us to become the Father's adopted heirs.

"Pray for us sinners." Humbly recognizing our spiritual poverty, we petition Mary to watch over us just as she watched over the child lying in the manger. Like Mary and Joseph, who were amazed to hear what shepherds told them, let us also hold and ponder in our hearts the hope that draws us from cold to warmth, darkness to light, barren winter branches to the leaves of spring all the days of our lives.

*Michael Dougherty*

**People and Prayers to Remember this Week**

_Readings of the Day_ —————————————————

Numbers 6.22-27          Galatians 4.4-7
Psalm 67                 Luke 2.16-21

**Responding to the Word**

**Mary reflected on all the ways God worked in her life. How
will I thank God for being present in my life this past year?**

_____

_____

_____

_____

_____

_____

_____

_____

_____

_____

_____

_____

## Final Thoughts ...

_____

_____

_____

_____

## Feasts this Week

# *Epiphany of the Lord*

I'VE OFTEN PONDERED whether the wise men were surprised by what they found at the end of their journey. They had left behind homes and safety and comfort, spending months following the star. And for what? To finally meet a mighty king living in a magnificent palace? Not even close. Instead, they found a child lying helpless in his mother's arms, living in the humblest of dwellings. Yet somehow the Magi were able to see beneath the child's poverty and vulnerability to recognize the one whom they had sought.

It makes me wonder how many times God comes to us in ways that may at first seem unexpected or even contradictory. While I certainly expected to feel God's presence in the birth of my child, I had no idea that I would sense – just as strongly – that same presence when I sat with my mother as she took her final breaths.

The feast of the Epiphany challenges us to be seekers as the wise men were seekers, to search for God and recognize God's presence wherever and whenever God chooses to reveal himself. When we discover one way God is present to us, wonderful! But we need to keep looking, always and everywhere, for other ways, too. Today we journey forth into the New Year with the Magi as our guides, always seeking and always searching for God's presence in the unexpected.

*Teresa Whalen Lux*

**People and Prayers to Remember this Week**

_Readings of the Day_ ————————————————

Isaiah 60.1-6                                   Ephesians 3.2-3a, 5-6
Psalm 72                                         Matthew 2.1-12

**Responding to the Word**

God's love is not limited and excludes no one. How can I
imitate God and include in my life someone I usually prefer
to stay apart from?

_____

_____

_____

_____

_____

_____

_____

_____

_____

_____

_____

_____

_____

_____

## Final Thoughts ...

_____

_____

_____

_____

## Feasts this Week

**January 9**   **The Baptism of the Lord**
**January 12**  **St Marguerite Bourgeoys (Canada)**
**January 13**  **St Hilary**

# 2nd Sunday in Ordinary Time

WHO EXACTLY IS this Jesus whose birth, epiphany, and baptism we have so recently celebrated? And what enduring relevance has God's entry into time for us?

The voices of Isaiah, John the Baptist, and Paul witness to the identity and mission of the Word become flesh. Isaiah sets the context for the incarnation as he anticipates a servant who will bring light and salvation to all. John affirms Jesus as the "Lamb of God," as the Son whose intimacy with God enables him to baptize with the Holy Spirit. Grace and peace are God's gifts to us through Jesus, Paul teaches. Anticipation, promise, prophecy are realized in and through the person of Jesus.

Isaiah, John, and Paul speak out of their experience, out of their lived relationship with God. We too are called to relationship with God. It is rather startling to hear that our call is to be saints – not saints as perfect, idealized, larger-than-life figures who are impossibly pious – but ordinary, everyday people who live as Christ-bearers, who recognize the dignity of all people, and who continue God's mission of love and compassion to the poor, the marginalized, to those most in need of light and healing.

With Isaiah, John, and Paul we are called to witness, to testify to the light through our words, our actions, our lives.

*Ella Allen*

**People and Prayers to Remember this Week**

*Readings of the Day* ——————————————————

Isaiah 49.3, 5-6                          1 Corinthians 1.1-3
Psalm 40                                  John 1.29-34

**Responding to the Word**

**John's task is to make Jesus known to others. How can I share my knowledge of Christ today?**

_____

_____

_____

_____

_____

_____

_____

_____

_____

_____

_____

_____

_____

_____

_____

## Final Thoughts …

_____

_____

_____

_____

## Feasts this Week

**January 17**  **St Anthony**
**January 20**  **St Fabian**
             **St Sebastian**
**January 21**  **St Agnes**

## SUNDAY JANUARY 22
Sunday of the Word of God
Week of Prayer for Christian Unity

# 3rd Sunday in Ordinary Time

THE LATIN ROOT of the word education means to draw out or to lead. It is appropriate, therefore, that in the same gospel passage in which we hear Jesus invite the apostles to follow him, we also hear of how he taught the people.

In Matthew's gospel, Christ begins his ministry by invoking the words of the prophet Isaiah, who makes use of the image of light. Light is a curious phenomenon for those of us living in the modern age. The invention of artificial lighting systems risks separating us from the natural light that is part of the beauty of creation. Some would argue that an increased reliance on artificial light may even be a cause of growing incidences of depression in our society – a condition often associated with darkness.

The gift of teaching is similar to the gift of light. Like the light that gently guides us along the path, a good teacher skillfully guides us to understanding. Christ calls each of us to our particular ministry through the actions of these capable and compassionate sisters and brothers.

Let us give thanks for all who have taught us the faith of our ancestors. May we be strengthened in our efforts to continue to teach what has been passed down to us, with praise and thanksgiving, acknowledging the light that leads our way.

*John O'Brien*

**People and Prayers to Remember this Week**

---

---

---

*Readings of the Day* ─────────────────────

Isaiah 9.1-4 (Canada)               1 Corinthians 1.10-13, 17-18
Isaiah 8.23 – 9.3 (USA)             Matthew 4.12-23
Psalm 27

**Responding to the Word**

Isaiah reminds us that God's presence is often recognized in what has been overlooked or neglected. Who or what might I not have noticed that is a source of God's presence?

---

---

---

---

---

---

---

---

_____

_____

_____

_____

_____

_____

_____

_____

_____

_____

_____

## Final Thoughts ...

_____

_____

_____

_____

## Feasts this Week

| January 23 | **Day of Prayer for the Legal Protection of Unborn Children (USA)** |
|---|---|
| | **St Vincent (USA)** |
| | **St Marianne Cope (USA)** |
| January 24 | **St Francis de Sales** |
| January 25 | **The Conversion of St Paul** |
| January 26 | **St Timothy & St Titus** |
| January 27 | **St Angela Merici** |
| January 28 | **St Thomas Aquinas** |

# *4th Sunday in Ordinary Time*

A LARGE, ORNATE chapel stands on the hill in Galilee now known as the Mount of the Beatitudes. There was nothing fancy, however, about the words Jesus uttered in what has come down to us as the Sermon on the Mount. "Blessed are the poor in spirit," he said, and for his listeners, who were possibly thinking that poor was the last thing they wanted to be, he proceeded to turn the world upside down. At the end of the long discourse, we are told that his listeners were "astounded." No wonder! Who wants to be meek, to be persecuted?

And yet – as we listen to this reading today, is there not something in Jesus's message that speaks to our hearts? Do we not hunger and thirst for righteousness, for something more soul-satisfying than the violence and injustice around us? Would we not welcome the chance to make peace, even in some small way, on this turbulent earth?

It may be that these words of Jesus turned some people away from him. But it could also be that those whose hearts he touched remained with him, those who recognized that in their poverty and insignificance there was still the capacity to make a difference in the world. Would I have been so inspired? May God grant me the desire to live today, in my own small way, by these words of Jesus.

*Mary Frances Coady*

**People and Prayers to Remember this Week**

*Readings of the Day* —————————————————

Zephaniah 2.3; 3.12-13          1 Corinthians 1.26-31
Psalm 146                       Matthew 5.1-12

**Responding to the Word**

Paul reminds us that human indicators are not what make us valuable in God's eyes. When have my evaluations of others been turned upside down by later events?

_____

_____

_____

_____

_____

_____

_____

_____

_____

_____

_____

_____

_____

_____

## Final Thoughts ...

_____

_____

_____

_____

## Feasts this Week

| | |
|---|---|
| **January 31** | **St John Bosco** |
| **February 2** | **The Presentation of the Lord** |
| **February 3** | **St Blaise** |
| | **St Ansgar** |

# *5th Sunday in Ordinary Time*

IMAGINE A WORLD without salt, without light – dull, dark, insipid, and lifeless. How often we take for granted these simple gifts of salt and light, symbols we ponder today as we reflect on the meaning of Christian discipleship.

For the people of Jesus' time salt was essential in a world without refrigeration. Its most delightful quality, though, is its ability to enhance the flavor of foods – not to give them a different taste, but to bring out the taste that is already there. A light is first and foremost something to be seen or it is of not much use, just as salt without flavor is useless.

These images of salt and light are part of Jesus' Sermon on the Mount, spoken to those who lack material goods and wait for the spiritual blessings promised by God. It is a happiness that reaches its fulfillment through Christ. This is not law. It is gospel, good news. The law challenges us to rely on our best efforts. The gospel confronts us with God's gifts and invites us to claim them as the basis for our life.

By our baptism, we are the light that shines in the darkness. We are the salt that gives new life to the world. This is what we celebrate in the Eucharist today.

*Sr. Mary Ellen Green, OP*

**People and Prayers to Remember this Week**

_Readings of the Day_

Isaiah 58.6-10                     1 Corinthians 2.1-5
Psalm 112                          Matthew 5.13-16

**Responding to the Word**

**Jesus calls his disciples the salt of the earth and light for the world. In what ways can I follow Jesus' teachings and be salt for the earth and light for the world?**

_____

_____

_____

_____

_____

_____

_____

_____

_____

_____

_____

_____

## Final Thoughts ...

_____

_____

_____

_____

## Feasts this Week

| | |
|---|---|
| **February 6** | **St Paul Miki & Companions** |
| **February 8** | **St Jerome Emiliani** |
| | **St Josephine Bakhita** |
| **February 10** | **St Scholastica** |
| **February 11** | **Our Lady of Lourdes** |

# 6th Sunday in Ordinary Time

IN THE FAST lane of life today, we are constantly challenged by a prevailing relativism – to make moral decisions on a case-by-case basis, and to put ourselves first, before considering others. As Christians, we must ask ourselves: how 'relative' – if at all – is God's kingdom? Today's readings help us to answer this question.

Sirach says that "Before each person are life and death, good and evil and whichever one chooses, that shall be given." There are no gray zones here, no room for individual interpretation. There is but one right choice. The Psalmist asserts, "Blessed are those whose way is blameless... who seek him with their whole heart." Our own idea of goodness pales beside the happiness and blessing that well up from the goodness of God.

In the gospel, we hear Jesus demand that we seek God whole-heartedly. It is not enough to comply with an intricate menu of rules, hoping for some kind of automatic redemption. The gospel of love is uncompromising: anger is akin to murder, lust is as destructive as adultery, and swearing falsely "comes from the evil one."

During today's Eucharist let us give thanks for the gift of wisdom, which Paul says is "not a wisdom of this age or of the rulers of this age, who are doomed to perish," but God's wisdom born of love and spoken through his Son, our redeemer.

*Beverley Illauq*

**People and Prayers to Remember this Week**

_____

_____

_____

*Readings of the Day* ———————————————

Sirach 15.15-20                    1 Corinthians 2.6-10
Psalm 119                          Matthew 5.17-37

**Responding to the Word**

**Paul cautions us about distinguishing worldly wisdom from God's wisdom. How has following God's wisdom helped me in my life?**

_____

_____

_____

_____

_____

_____

_____

_____

_____

_____

_____

_____

_____

_____

_____

_____

_____

_____

_____

_____

_____

_____

_____

## Final Thoughts ...

_____

_____

_____

_____

## Feasts this Week

**February 14**   **St Cyril & St Methodius**
**February 17**   **The Seven Holy Founders of the Servite Order**

# 7th Sunday in Ordinary Time

WHAT A DAUNTING challenge Jesus puts to us today. He tells us we must love and pray for people who not only don't love us, but who wish us harm and even work against us. Is that even possible? Maybe there are one or two saints who could pull it off, but most of us would find it too hard to resist the urge for payback when we feel we have been wronged. Yet Jesus is very clear: he is asking us to be perfect!

But before giving up in dismay – after all, who is perfect? – let's look at what else Jesus tells us. Every single day, the sun rises and gives warmth and light to everyone and everything: the young, the old, the sick, the healthy – and the good and the bad. The rain, too, doesn't fall only in deserving places. It just falls – and cleans and nourishes whatever and whomever it lands on. Neither the sunshine nor the rain makes judgments about who should receive them and who should not. They simply offer to the world the goodness that is at the heart of their being.

So we, too, should hold back on making judgments, no matter how appealing that might be. Instead, we are asked simply to offer our inner goodness to the world – kindness, generosity, prayer, forgiveness, love. This is not easy, but who said being a follower of Jesus would be easy?

*Patrick Gallagher*

**People and Prayers to Remember this Week**

_Readings of the Day_

Leviticus 19.1-2, 17-18
Psalm 103

1 Corinthians 3.16-23
Matthew 5.38-48

**Responding to the Word**

**Jesus challenges us to pray for our enemies and persecutors. How do I respond to those who hurt or offend me?**

_____

_____

_____

_____

_____

_____

_____

_____

_____

_____

_____

_____

_____

_____

**Final Thoughts ...**

_____

_____

_____

_____

## Feasts this Week

**February 21**   **St Peter Damian**
**February 22**   **Ash Wednesday**
**February 23**   **St Polycarp**

# *Ash Wednesday*

I'VE GOT MY skinny jeans tucked away in the back of my closet because I'm going to wear them again. I am. On optimistic days, I take them down and shimmy them on. Part-way, at least. The resulting tantrum isn't pretty. I make excuses, lay blame, get angry, and cry – all stages of grief. I suppose I'm grieving the image I had of myself. But the whole experience makes me look at that honest reflection and ask: Who am I kidding?

Today's gospel invites us to take a similar look at our piety. To pinch that spiritual flab and honestly ask: Who am I kidding?

Bible studies, prayer groups, volunteering, fundraising, and committees – from the outside, our actions may seem like we are in great spiritual shape. We've convinced ourselves, and maybe even a few others, of our spiritual strength. But on the inside, if we feel resentful, unappreciated, and downright weary – perhaps we are doing those right things for the wrong reasons.

Today, Jesus calls us to look honestly at our motives for generosity, sacrificing, and prayer. We may have good intentions, but sometimes they can be overtaken by our secret desires to impress and maintain that false image. Jesus challenges us to beware. Re-focus and re-commit to the Father who sees all in secret.

Ash Wednesdays and skinny jeans – moments of truth that inspire humility and change.

*Caroline Pignat*

**People and Prayers to Remember this Week**

_Readings of the Day_ ────────────────

Joel 2.12-18

Psalm 51

2 Corinthians 5.20 – 6.2

Matthew 6.1-6, 16-18

**Responding to the Word**

**Jesus warns against hypocritical behavior. What do I need to do to match my words with my actions?**

**Final Thoughts ...**

# *1st Sunday of Lent*

THERE IS A place deep inside us where we know what is right. We hold certain beliefs and values. But knowing is one thing and doing is another. It's about integrity, living what we believe.

Jesus struggles to maintain that integrity. He knows that his mission – to teach the way of eternal life – will be far from easy. Yet, he is baptized and follows the Spirit into the "wilderness" to fast, pray, and prepare. The "wilderness" is a physical place away from cities and people, but also a spiritual space where we become stronger by facing our inner turmoil and overcoming temptation.

Jesus is tempted to turn stones into bread, just to prove his own power. But he chooses cooperation with God over defiance. He is also tempted to test God's saving power by jumping off a cliff. But he resists, knowing there is no reason to doubt God's goodness. He is even tempted to succumb to an offer of material wealth that would jeopardize his relationship with God. But he remembers that God alone, the Creator of all life, is worthy of worship and service.

Often, just when we begin a new mission or a difficult commitment, the temptation to defy or ignore God is strongest. As we enter the "wilderness" of Lent, struggling to live what we believe, let us remember that just as angels came to comfort Jesus, so will we be comforted.

*Ferdinanda Van Gennip*

**People and Prayers to Remember this Week**

_____

_____

_____

*Readings of the Day* ———————————————————

Genesis 2.7-9, 16-18, 25; 3.1-7       Romans 5.12-19
Psalm 51                              Matthew 4.1-11

**Responding to the Word**

Paul reminds us that we have a new chance for a sinless life as Jesus' gift to us. What can I do today to imitate Jesus' generosity?

_____

_____

_____

_____

_____

_____

_____

_____

_____

Final Thoughts ...

Feasts this Week

**February 27**  **St Gregory of Narek**
**March 3**  **St Katharine Drexel (USA)**
**March 4**  **St Casimir**

# 2nd Sunday of Lent

THE THREE READINGS for today speak of calling. In the first reading, God called Abraham, asking him to leave all and go with his wife, Sarah, to a strange land, promising him land and descendants. In faith, following this strange new voice, Abraham went, becoming the father of Jews, Christians, and Muslims.

In the second reading, Paul calls us to join with him "in suffering for the gospel." The gospel is the good news of God's love for each of us. What do good news and love have to do with hardship? Love and suffering are the two sides of human experience. Couples enter into marriage because of love, and experience the hardships of a close relationship.

Parents bring children into the world because of love, and face the hardship of raising these children to adulthood. Singles often long for love, and face the hardship of loneliness.

In the gospel, God calls Jesus up to a high mountain where heaven is opened to him. Jesus converses with Moses and Elijah about his "passing" that is to take place in Jerusalem. In other words, his crucifixion, his hardship, is the manifestation of God's unconditional love for each of us.

God called, Abraham went. God called, Jesus went to Jerusalem and to his death. God calls me. Can I discern the good news of divine love in the hardship of my life?

*Jim Wolff*

**People and Prayers to Remember this Week**

_Readings of the Day_ —————————————————

Genesis 12.1-4                    2 Timothy 1.8b-10
Psalm 33                          Matthew 17.1-9

**Responding to the Word**

**Abraham gave up much to do as the Lord commanded. What must I give up this Lent to let God take up more space in my life?**

_____

_____

_____

_____

_____

_____

_____

_____

_____

_____

_____

_____

_____

_____

_____

_____

## Final Thoughts …

_____

_____

_____

## Feasts this Week

**March 7    St Perpetua & St Felicity**
**March 8    St John of God**
**March 9    St Frances of Rome**

# 3rd Sunday of Lent

HAVE YOU EVER lived in or traveled to the desert or to places where water is scarce or unfit to drink? Those of us who have, know what it is like to feel truly parched with no immediate expectation that our thirst will be quenched. We can readily identify with the Israelite people in the reading from Exodus, who, having fled Egypt, now find themselves in the desert, desperately in need of fresh, clean, reinvigorating water, knowing that they must move forward but fearful that they will die of thirst.

For Christians, Lent is that dry, parched, desert time in the liturgical year when we recall the 40 days Jesus spent in the desert in preparation for his ministry. In our parishes we experience this desert time when we refrain from pouring baptismal waters. The prominence of water in this week's readings seems to drive home to us that we are still a long way away from the flowing waters of our Easter celebrations. We must persevere.

Along with the catechumens and the candidates journeying to the Rites of Initiation, we take this opportunity to experience the unquenched thirst that comes with fasting and deep prayer. We pray that we might be purified, enlightened, and truly prepared to bathe in the new waters of Easter. It is only then that we will be restored and brought to new life in water and the Spirit.

*Connie Paré*

**People and Prayers to Remember this Week**

_____

_____

_____

*Readings of the Day* ——————————————————————

Exodus 17.3-7
Psalm 95

Romans 5.1-2, 5-8
John 4.5-42

**Responding to the Word**

**The people grumble because they think Moses and God are not taking care of them enough. What causes me to grumble about God's care for me?**

_____

_____

_____

_____

_____

_____

_____

_____

_____

_____

_____

_____

_____

_____

_____

_____

_____

_____

_____

_____

_____

_____

_____

_____

_____

## Final Thoughts ...

_____

_____

_____

_____

## Feasts this Week

**March 17    St Patrick**
**March 18    St Cyril of Jerusalem**

# *4th Sunday of Lent*

TODAY WE HEAR of Samuel visiting Jesse to choose the next king. Samuel makes his own choice based on outward appearances, but God let him know that the Lord sees into the heart. David is anointed because his heart is for God. David's psalm, the "Lord is my Shepherd," proves his trust in God.

In the gospel, Jesus heals a man who was blind from birth so that the works of God are made visible through him. The man, believing in Jesus and desiring to please God, can see! By his faith he passed from darkness into light.

During Lent we consciously walk in the light, making our hearts and lives pleasing to God. We allow our hearts to be open, like the blind man, letting God's light and love heal us. We see more clearly and become more sensitive to fulfilling our own callings. What is our current spiritual vision? 20/20? Are we near- or far-sighted, or do we a have few blind spots? It is easy to lose sight of good intentions when faced with the world's darkness, but when God's light dwells within our hearts, we overcome what may be stifled and radiate Christ's light, love, and peace.

Let us give thanks for those being called to enter into the Christian faith, for they desire to live as children of the light. As we welcome them, may we together radiate the Light of Christ.

*Kelly Anne Mantler*

**People and Prayers to Remember this Week**

*Readings of the Day* ————————————————————

1 Samuel 16.1b, 6-7, 10-13          Ephesians 5.8-14
Psalm 23                            John 9.1-41

**Responding to the Word**

God looks beyond the appearances into the heart of each
person. How can I get beyond the appearances when
meeting and dealing with others?

_____

_____

_____

_____

_____

_____

_____

_____

_____

_____

_____

_____

_____

_____

**Final Thoughts ...**

_____

_____

_____

_____

**Feasts this Week**

**March 20    St Joseph**
**March 23    St Turibius of Mogrovejo**
**March 25    The Annunciation of the Lord**

# 5th Sunday of Lent

LIFE AND DEATH; hope and despair; the anguish of waiting – today's gospel is awash with gut-wrenching emotion. Yet while reading the story of the death and resurrection of Lazarus, I sit content and self-satisfied. My heart remains indifferent and untouched. I know the ending to this drama and am expecting Easter.

Then I ponder. What is resurrection? What does it mean in my daily life? I remember a day last winter. Tethered to a trusted companion, belted securely into a "sit ski," I sat poised to take my first downhill ski run. As we took off, an explosion of joy filled my body. Handicapped since birth, I had never experienced such freedom... such wild abandon... such present-moment living! I squealed with child-like wonder as my toque took flight in the wind. A piece of my soul, long ago buried, was resurrected. That day I was unbound and set free.

When I think of my time on the hill, I realize that the experience of resurrection is a verb... a dynamic, vibrant, forever-in-motion verb! Each day Jesus yearns to reach down and unbind me from many death-like experiences. With Lazarus I can now hear the voice of Jesus calling me to full life. Willingly I stand straight and tall as Jesus unbinds me from that which hinders. Come! Experience resurrection as a verb!

*Karen Johnson*

**People and Prayers to Remember this Week**

_____

_____

_____

*Readings of the Day* —————————————————

Ezekiel 37.12-14          Romans 8.8-11
Psalm 130                 John 11.1-45

**Responding to the Word**

Christ and the Holy Spirit dwell in me to give life. What signs of their presence have I noticed, especially this Lent?

_____

_____

_____

_____

_____

_____

_____

_____

_____

_____

**Final Thoughts ...**

# *Passion (Palm) Sunday*

TODAY'S READINGS ENCOURAGE us to reflect on our gifts and how we use them for others and for the glory of God. Each of us could nod in agreement when Isaiah acknowledges: "The Lord God has given me the tongue of a teacher." God has blessed each of us this way, Isaiah continues, so that we "may know how to sustain the weary with a word." Our gifts are to be shared and life-giving.

Paul encourages us to use our voices to confess that Jesus is Lord. We are called to emulate the total self-giving of Jesus in every gift, phone call, love note, and message of concern we convey to those in need.

The disciples used their voices to exclaim their innocence. Jesus used his to speak the words that would ensure his life among us. "Take, eat; this is my Body." Then, taking the cup, "Drink from it, all of you; for this is my Blood of the covenant, which is poured out for many for the forgiveness of sins."

Don't hold back and bite your tongue. Use it to speak a word of God. Use it to confess that Jesus is Lord! Use it as God does, to bless and create a way to continue God's life among us and within us. Let us use our well-trained voices for the benefit of our neighbor and for the glory of God.

*Sr. Martha Alken, OP*

People and Prayers to Remember this Week

_____

_____

_____

*Readings of the Day* ————————————————

Matthew 21.1-11 (Procession)    Philippians 2.6-11
Isaiah 50.4-7                   Matthew 26.14 – 27.66
Psalm 22

Responding to the Word

**Paul encourages us to imitate Christ's humility. Which area or relationship in my life needs more humility?**

_____

_____

_____

_____

_____

_____

_____

_____

_____

**Final Thoughts ...**

# Holy Thursday

ASK ANYONE WITH memory problems – not to be able to remember is, at best, deeply frustrating. At worst, whole parts of one's life and identity simply cease to be. This day, this remembering of the Lord's Supper, is vital to our life, identity, and mission as Christians. Today we remember one of the most intimate, moving, and crucial moments of Jesus' life.

Our remembering is fourfold: Jesus shielding us from death, opening us to new life; foot-washing, which is the test of our discipleship and intimacy with Jesus; Eucharist, which makes real the saving death and resurrection of Jesus; love, which fulfills our life's purpose in bringing the reign of God to our world, in our lifetime.

Remembering must be grasped, solidified, made tangible, lest we forget and risk slipping into a kind of amnesia of the will and spirit.

Remembering isn't confined to church. Unless we remember every day in our lives – in our choices for justice and the poor, in our loving to the end of our energy and time, in our washing of the feet of the homeless and the hungry and the others around whom we are uncomfortable – unless our remembering is active every day, we are all talk and no action.

Remember with the community this night. Remember in your taking the bread and drinking the cup. Remember with your life... remember.

*Sr. Phyllis Giroux, SC*

**People and Prayers to Remember this Week**

*Readings of the Day*

Exodus 12.1-8, 11-14              1 Corinthians 11.23-26
Psalm 116                         John 13.1-15

**Responding to the Word**

The sacrifice of the Passover lamb expresses the people's complete dedication to God and the desire to share life with God. What sacrifice must I make to rededicate myself to God today?

_____

_____

_____

_____

_____

_____

_____

_____

_____

_____

_____

_____

_____

_____

_____

_____

_____

_____

**Final Thoughts …**

_____

_____

_____

_____

# *Good Friday*

SUFFERING REMAINS A tremendous mystery for each one of us. It raises a wide and dreadful series of questions: Why is there suffering? Why me? Why do the innocent suffer? Is suffering willed by God? Permitted by him? Why does God seem so distant, hiding? Is God powerless towards suffering?

These are daring questions. But today is the day in the liturgical year in which these questions are given full attention. Good Friday, in all its solemnity and intensity, is the day to let these questions resound. Good Friday is essential. It teaches us the humility of a God who has not feared to take on himself the immensity of our human sorrows, sufferings, and tragedies.

The cross of Jesus stands as a reminder of how serious God is about this matter that troubles us so much. On the cross, Jesus bears our questions and brings them to his Father's attention. At the same time, the cross stands as the most powerful sign of hope. In Jesus, God reveals himself both as a suffering and a loving God. It is not the suffering of Jesus that saved the world, but the love of God manifested in Jesus now on the cross and loving his own to the end. It is also our love for those around us who suffer that will bring them comfort and hope, and redeem their suffering.

*Jean-Pierre Prévost*

**People and Prayers to Remember this Week**

_Readings of the Day_

Isaiah 52.13 – 53.12          Hebrews 4.14-16; 5.7-9
Psalm 31                      John 18.1 – 19.42

**Responding to the Word**

Isaiah's suffering servant foreshadows the rejection and suffering of Jesus. What suffering is most difficult for me to deal with now in my life?

**Final Thoughts ...**

# *Easter Vigil*

As WE BEGIN tonight's Easter Vigil liturgy, our hearts are stirred by the lighting of the new fire, and by having our candles lit to symbolize the risen Christ, Light of the world. The singing of the Exsultet lifts our spirits, and we cherish hearing again the stories of our origins and ancestors in faith.

Tonight's gospel invites us to go with the two Marys, so anxious to visit the tomb where Jesus is buried. Who would have expected that they would encounter an earthquake, the tomb stone rolled back, and angels appearing to say, "He is not here; he has been raised!" In fear and joy they run to tell the disciples, when suddenly they meet Jesus. Overwhelmed, they embrace his feet and worship him, their hearts telling them something wondrously new is happening.

Easter is not about passively contemplating an empty tomb. It's an invitation to encounter the risen Christ, to believe, to rejoice, and to share the good news. By his resurrection, Jesus reaches out to all who are entombed in the world, setting every heart free from sin and death to embrace his gift of new life.

Tonight, in faith and hope, let us renew our baptismal promises to the risen Lord, in whom death is no more; life is eternal. Let us celebrate in joy his spirit of love among us, transforming all humanity – indeed creation itself.

*Rev. Michael Traher, SFM*

**People and Prayers to Remember this Week**

*Readings of the Day* —————————————————

Genesis 1.1 – 2.2

Psalm 104 or Psalm 33

Genesis 22.1-18

Psalm 16

Exodus 14.15-31; 15.20, 1

Exodus 15

Isaiah 54.5-14

Psalm 30

Isaiah 55.1-11

Isaiah 12

Baruch 3.9-15, 32 – 4.4

Psalm 19

Ezekiel 36.16-17a, 18-28

Psalm 42 or Psalm 51

Romans 6.3-11

Psalm 118

Matthew 28.1-10

**Responding to the Word**

**Jesus tells his disciples not to be afraid. What fears must I overcome to witness to Christ today?**

**Final Thoughts ...**

# *Easter Sunday*

IT IS EASTER! Easter is about life: life where we least expect to find it, life that overcomes the power of evil and death. Today's gospel hints at this in showing us the disciples looking for Jesus in the tomb. Mary Magdalene had seen Jesus die on the cross and wanted to honor him one last time. She looked for Jesus who had died and found only emptiness. Peter and the other disciple saw only the linen that had wrapped Jesus' body. There was no sign of life.

The disciples were invited to change their way of thinking: to see life in a new way, with new eyes. Mary recognized Jesus when he addressed her by name, but she still had to learn that although Jesus was alive and present to her, his risen life was different. She had to let go of what had been familiar and accept Jesus' new way of being with her. Death had changed everything, but it did not extinguish the life that is God's gift.

As Christians we are Easter people, people who support, uphold, and proclaim life. Like Mary and Peter and the other witnesses to the resurrection, we are invited to recognize life in new ways, even where all seems to be darkness, for our God is the God of resurrection, the God of life.

*Sr. Barbara Bozak, CSJ*

**People and Prayers to Remember Today**

_____

_____

_____

*Readings of the Day* ————————————————

Acts 10.34a, 37-43
Psalm 118
Colossians 3.1-4
or 1 Corinthians 5.6b-8

John 20.1-18
or Matthew 28.1-10
or Luke 24.13-35

**Responding to the Word**

**The disciples found it hard to believe because they did not understand the Scriptures. How can I use the Scriptures so that my belief might be stronger?**

_____

_____

_____

_____

_____

_____

_____

**Final Thoughts ...**

# 2nd Sunday of Easter

TODAY'S GOSPEL MIGHT make us feel unsettled – and not only because, like Thomas, we sometimes struggle with doubt in our relationship with God. We may also feel uncomfortable with the invitation Jesus extends to us via Thomas, to touch the wounds of one another and to bring healing to those wounds.

Thomas is preoccupied with his confusion of emotions. His reaction to the news of the resurrection is born out of his feelings of grief, fear, hurt, and anger. He challenges Jesus, throwing down the gauntlet with a threat that, without seeing and touching the wounds, he will not believe. Jesus accepts the challenge, guiding Thomas to feel the wounds of the crucifixion. Thomas is overcome with joy.

John vividly portrays Jesus' wounds as large and gaping. Thomas' hand can fit into Jesus' side; his finger can fit into the wounds on Jesus' hands. The fleshiness of this image gently, but insistently, challenges us to become bearers of Christ's peace. John invites us to respond to Jesus, who is calling us out of our hurts and fears to what the second reading calls "a new birth into a living hope."

Today, let us celebrate the hope that resolves doubt and heals wounds. Let us celebrate with the same joy that made Thomas proclaim, "My Lord and my God!" Let us be, like the first disciples, a living hope to the world.

*Louise McEwan*

**People and Prayers to Remember Today**

*Readings of the Day* —————————————————

**Acts 2.42-47**
**Psalm 118**

**1 Peter 1.3-9**
**John 20.19-31**

**Responding to the Word**

**God's mercy or compassion offers us new life. How can my compassion for others give them new life?**

_____

_____

_____

_____

_____

_____

_____

_____

_____

_____

_____

_____

_____

_____

_____

## Final Thoughts ...

_____

_____

_____

_____

## Feasts this Week

**April 17**  **St Kateri Tekakwitha (Canada)**
**April 18**  **Bl Marie-Anne Blondin (Canada)**
**April 21**  **St Anselm**

# 3rd Sunday of Easter

HAVE YOU EVER had an "aha!" moment? It can be quite rare, but when we get one, we know it. It comes as an instant recognition, a realization, a light dawning – we suddenly "get it," sometimes after a long period of seeming quite dense. And that can feel awfully good.

Psychologists are looking increasingly at what happens when our brain and body make a "mindful" connection. Athletes call this "being in the zone" – that perfect moment when you can do no wrong. Mystics understand that this connection takes place in the soul. This is the sort of epiphany the disciples experienced while walking on the road to Emmaus with Jesus.

There are two key elements of the miracle that occurred on that first Easter, and they remain with us to this day in the gift of the Mass – sharing the Word and sharing the Eucharist. After Jesus shared the Scriptures with the disciples, "when he was at the table with them, he took bread, blessed and broke it, and gave it to them. Then their eyes were opened, and they recognized him; and he vanished from their sight."

Think about it! If we open ourselves up to the miracle of Christ in the Word and in the Eucharist, here and now, he is here with us again. And that is a miracle.

*Patrick M. Doyle*

**People and Prayers to Remember Today**

_____

_____

_____

*Readings of the Day* ———————————————

Acts 2.14, 22-33                    1 Peter 1.17-21
Psalm 16                            Luke 24.13-35

**Responding to the Word**

**Peter urges us to conduct ourselves with reverence. What can I do to show my reverence for God and others?**

_____

_____

_____

_____

_____

_____

_____

_____

_____

_____

_____

_____

_____

_____

_____

_____

_____

_____

_____

_____

_____

_____

## Final Thoughts ...

_____

_____

_____

_____

## Feasts this Week

**April 24** **St Fidelis of Sigmaringen**
**April 25** **St Mark**
**April 26** **Our Lady of Good Counsel (Canada)**
**April 28** **St Peter Chanel**
         **St Louis Grignion de Montfort**
**April 29** **St Catherine of Siena**

# 4th Sunday of Easter

In PASTORAL CARE, we often refer to "companions on the journey." These are the people who travel with us, particularly when we rely on another person for strength, guidance, and comfort. In Christian life, we model our role of companion after Jesus Christ.

In today's readings, Jesus is presented as a shepherd. We know the shepherd as the one who stands between his sheep and all harm. Likewise, we know Jesus as the One who lays down his life for each of us. We know the shepherd as the one who leads the way, choosing the safest path. Likewise, we know Jesus as our guide who directs us on the right path, protecting us with his Spirit. We know the shepherd as the one whose voice his sheep recognize and follow. Likewise, we know Jesus as the one who calls us each by name.

In our hectic lives, when many voices call out and many paths present themselves, and we truly need a companion on the journey, where do we encounter our shepherd? We encounter him today, in this remembrance and celebration of Jesus' sacrifice for us. It is here that our relationship with Jesus is deepened and nurtured. But this is only the beginning. The companion we meet here journeys with us each day, protecting, guiding, and calling us forth by name that we might have life and have it to the fullest.

*Shelley Kuiack*

**People and Prayers to Remember this Week**

_Readings of the Day_ —————————————————

Acts 2.14a, 36-41                    1 Peter 2.20b-25
Psalm 23                             John 10.1-10

**Responding to the Word**

**Personal conversion and baptism into the community are expected of new followers. What changes in my life do I seek during this Easter season?**

_____

_____

_____

_____

_____

_____

_____

_____

_____

_____

_____

_____

## Final Thoughts ...

_____

_____

_____

_____

## Feasts this Week

| | |
|---|---|
| May 1 | **St Joseph the Worker** |
| | **St Pius V (Canada)** |
| May 2 | **St Athanasius** |
| May 3 | **St Philip & St James** |
| May 4 | **Bl Marie-Léonie Paradis (Canada)** |
| May 6 | **St François de Laval (Canada)** |

# 5th Sunday of Easter

TAKE A DEEP breath before you read today's gospel. What you are about to read leaves reality TV in the dust. You are about to receive the ultimate challenge. Telling his disciples that he will soon be leaving them and going to be with the Father, Jesus says, "The one who believes in me will also do the works that I do and, in fact, will do greater works than these."

There you have it. We who are followers of Jesus are called not only to believe in him and to speak the good news of salvation to others: we are also expected to do what Jesus did. We all know what that looks like, and the list is quite long: heal the sick, comfort those in pain, protect the weak and vulnerable, embrace the poor, eat with sinners, defend the rights of those who are victimized, denounce injustice, and more. The task becomes more daunting when we realize that we ourselves are sinners. We may believe, but without the power and endless love that form the essence of the Son of God, how is it possible to do greater works than Jesus did?

People in Africa have a saying: The path is made by walking. Each time we show our faith by doing the things that Jesus did, we take another step toward being better believers than we were before. A challenge, yes. Possible? Without a doubt!

*Susan Eaton*

**People and Prayers to Remember this Week**

---

*Readings of the Day* ————————————————

Acts 6.1-7                          1 Peter 2.4-9
Psalm 33                            John 14.1-12

**Responding to the Word**

**The Twelve call others to service in the community. What new service can I offer to my community?**

## Final Thoughts ...

## Feasts this Week

**May 8**  **Bl Catherine of St Augustine (Canada)**
**May 10**  **St John of Avila**
  **St Damien de Veuster (USA)**
**May 12**  **St Nereus & St Achilleus**
  **St Pancras**
**May 13**  **Our Lady of Fatima**

# 6th Sunday of Easter

IN THESE WEEKS after Easter we are making our way through the Acts of the Apostles. We should really read it as the acts of the Holy Spirit, enabling his disciples to become like Christ. We see them preaching like Christ and working miracles like his. In today's reading we see them being persecuted by the same people who crucified Christ and, just as the Cross gives the gospel its power, so the persecution of the apostles spreads the good news around the world.

In Samaria, Peter and John bestow the Spirit upon those who have been baptized into Christ. They have the power to do this because Christ has already bestowed the Spirit on them. John's gospel repeatedly emphasizes that Christ's first and greatest gift is the gift of the Spirit who acts as our advocate and speaks through and for us. The Paraclete, the Advocate, is thus the Spirit of truth who leads believers into all truth. The Spirit dwells within our hearts, for the Spirit is love who unites us with the Father in Christ.

Next Sunday we will celebrate the Lord's Ascension. We should not think of the Spirit as a replacement for Christ, but rather as God uniting us with the Christ who lives in glory in the union of the Father. It is the glorification of this Christ that we celebrate in this Eucharist by the power of the Spirit.

*Jennifer Cooper*

**People and Prayers to Remember this Week**

_____

_____

_____

*Readings of the Day* ───────────────────

Acts 8.5-8, 14-17                    1 Peter 3.15-18
Psalm 66                             John 14.15-21

**Responding to the Word**

**The crowds respond with joy to the words and signs that reveal Christ. What has caused me to rejoice during this Easter season?**

_____

_____

_____

_____

_____

_____

_____

_____

_____

_____

_____

_____

_____

_____

_____

_____

_____

_____

_____

_____

_____

_____

_____

## Final Thoughts ...

_____

_____

_____

_____

## Feasts this Week

**May 15  St Isidore (USA)**
**May 18  St John I**
**The Ascension of the Lord (in some dioceses of the USA)**
**May 20  St Bernardine of Siena**

# The Ascension of the Lord

THE LAST FIVE verses of Matthew's gospel are tinged with great solemnity. The gathering of the eleven disciples takes place on a mountain — a great place to encounter God and be sent out for a mission. The encounter with the Risen Jesus reported by Matthew is not only the encounter of a lifetime for the disciples, but also the end of Jesus of Nazareth's earthly presence among us. Now in this momentous and historic farewell, while claiming total authority from God, Jesus gives us as well the assurance he will be forever God-with-us, the Emmanuel.

But what about the disciples and their commissioning? Their initial reaction to encountering the Risen Jesus is, to say the least, mixed. It is to these disciples — split between faith and doubt — that Jesus says: "Go therefore and make disciples of all nations!" At this stage, we would have liked to hear about the disciples' reaction to such great commissioning. Matthew has decided otherwise. By remaining silent on the immediate reaction of the eleven and thus leaving his gospel open-ended, Matthew is inviting all his readers up to this day to make Jesus' commissioning of the disciples their own and to tell the unwritten part of the story. Matthew wanted us to be part of that story: it is now up to each one of us to testify to the world to the unfailing and loving presence of Emmanuel.

*Jean-Pierre Prévost*

*The 7th Sunday of Easter is celebrated in some dioceses of the USA today. Refer to p. 99.

**People and Prayers to Remember this Week**

*Readings of the Day*

Acts 1.1-11        Ephesians 1.17-23

Psalm 47        Matthew 28.16-20

**Responding to the Word**

**Jesus sends us to make disciples of others. What can I do to bring someone closer to Christ today?**

_____

_____

_____

_____

_____

_____

_____

_____

_____

_____

_____

## Final Thoughts ...

_____

_____

_____

_____

## Feasts this Week

**May 22**  **St Rita of Cascia**
**May 24**  **Bl Louis-Zépherin Moreau (Canada)**
**May 25**  **St Bede the Venerable**
          **St Gregory VII**
          **St Mary Magdalene de'Pazzi**
**May 26**  **St Philip Neri**
**May 27**  **St Augustine of Canterbury**

# 7th Sunday of Easter

AT THE END of his words at the Last Supper, Jesus stops preaching his final teachings and he pours himself out in prayer to the Father for the disciples. Before the agony in the garden, before the betrayals, before the suffering, he names the glory of doing what the Father asks. He places those who have loved him, those who have given everything to follow him, gently in the hands of his Father.

When Jesus can no longer hold us himself, he entrusts us to the One who can.

Everything that God asks of us in this life is bigger than we are. All the things worth doing for the kingdom go beyond us: ministry, parenting, justice work, prophecy, teaching, healing. It's all a participation in something so much bigger. Jesus shows us how we should understand and live out our calling and then how we hand it back to the Creator of it all, when our time comes to leave the world.

Jesus can walk into his betrayal, his own longing to live, his suffering and death because he has handed back to God what is God's. He gives us back because we belong to the Father.

Almighty and ever-living God, this is the gift of our calling: we are participants in your mission. We are entrusted with flames and moments, sparks and possibilities, lifetimes and graces for a time. When we have nurtured them with our love, may we give them back to you because they were never ours, but always yours. Amen.

*Leah Perrault*

**People and Prayers to Remember this Week**

*Readings of the Day*

Acts 1.12-14                    1 Peter 4.13-16
Psalm 27                        John 17.1-11a

**Responding to the Word**

**Jesus prays for the unity among his disciples. What can I do to promote unity in my relationships?**

**Final Thoughts ...**

# *Pentecost Sunday*

EVER SINCE I was a child, I have been intrigued by the events of Pentecost day. How was it possible for so many people to hear the message in their own language? How could the disciples even make themselves heard in such a crowd?

But the mechanics are not important, I realize. After all, what does it matter how it happened? The key point is that through no power of their own, the disciples were able to speak to a crowd of people from all over the ancient world. And through no power of their own, the people gathered were able to understand the disciples' words.

As the Bible teaches us, God always knows how to speak in ways that people will understand. Through the Scriptures, through loving relationships, through the Eucharist, through prayer of all kinds, through beauty, even through silence, God speaks. God's people – whether they realize it or not – are enfolded in a life-changing, life-giving message of hope.

All we need to do is be present and open our ears and our hearts. Then, as the disciples gathered in the upper room found out, Jesus will appear among us, bringing us God's peace and the power of the Holy Spirit. Filled with the Spirit, we can unlock the doors that imprison us and break free to share the good news with everyone we meet.

*Anne Louise Mahoney*

**People and Prayers to Remember this Week**

---

*Readings of the Day* ——————————————————

Acts 2.1-11                          1 Corinthians 12.3b-7, 12-13
Psalm 104                            John 20.19-23

**Responding to the Word**

**The disciples are changed by their contact with God's Holy Spirit. What changes has God brought about in me during this Easter season?**

_____

_____

_____

_____

_____

_____

_____

_____

_____

_____

_____

_____

_____

## Final Thoughts ...

_____

_____

_____

_____

## Feasts this Week

**May 29**  **The Blessed Virgin Mary, Mother of the Church**
**May 31**  **The Visitation of the Blessed Virgin Mary**
**June 1**  **St Justin**
**June 2**  **St Marcellinus & St Peter**
**June 3**  **St Charles Lwanga & Companions**

# The Most Holy Trinity

"GOD SO LOVED the world..." Love is the first step in the dance, and God always takes the lead. It's the dance into which we have been introduced at our baptism: life in the Trinity.

If you want to begin to approach the mystery of the Trinity as anything other than a mathematical equation, begin with love. It's love poured out, love given, love received and shared that is the essence of this mystery. Then, think love in motion – not a static equation, but love moving between persons whom we name as Father, Son, and Spirit. Think of a dance between three equal lovers who have nothing else to do but love. That's the essence of Trinitarian life.

We tend to think of the Trinity as "up there" (or over there) – distant from us (a distance that absolves us from any obligation to participate!). But Trinity, in fact, is our home address. We live in the Trinity. From the time of our baptism, we have been caught up in the dance that is love poured out, handed over, returned, shared. This love is our highest calling, our source of morality, and our greatest delight.

That humanity is invited into the communion of love that is the God of Jesus Christ boggles our minds. But don't get caught in the boggle. Ignore your two left feet. Let God lead you in the best dance of your life.

*Bernadette Gasslein*

**People and Prayers to Remember this Week**

_____

_____

_____

*Readings of the Day* ——————————————————

**Exodus 34.4b-6, 8-9**          **2 Corinthians 13.11-13**
**Daniel 3**                     **John 3.16-18**

**Responding to the Word**

**Jesus did not come to condemn us but to teach us how to love. When am I more ready to condemn than to love? Why?**

_____

_____

_____

_____

_____

_____

_____

_____

_____

_____

**Final Thoughts ...**

**Feasts this Week**

**June 5   St Boniface**
**June 6   St Norbert**
**June 9   St Ephrem**

# *The Body and Blood of Christ*

CHRIST'S BODY CONTINUES to be broken and his blood shed today; we have yet to accept and cooperate with the presence and activity of Jesus in the world. In our Church, our world, and our earth Christ is suffering: in broken relationships and exclusion; among people at war and cities destroyed; in our polluted waters and soil; in inequitable access to resources. A message of hope is needed, a new way of living in the face of overwhelming need.

Christ gave us his body and blood, and continues to do so in every Eucharist, that we might be formed into his very self. He offers himself as food for our growth, food that prepares us for struggle and for loving, food that forms us as one body to live in solidarity, sharing so that each one has what is needed for life.

Christ's body is given and his blood outpoured when we give of ourselves – in families, for a friend or neighbor, in communities and organizations, in the workplace. Wherever and whenever we offer a kind word or gesture; provide support for struggling people; give aid for the poor, hungry, and homeless; whenever we advocate for justice: here, too, Christ is made present for others – healing, loving, and sharing.

To eat of his body is to give ourselves for others and to live in Christ. In this we will have eternal life.

*Sr. Carmen Diston, IBVM*

**People and Prayers to Remember this Week**

_____

_____

_____

*Readings of the Day* —————————————————————

Deuteronomy 8.2-3, 14-16          1 Corinthians 10.16-17
Psalm 147                        John 6.51-59

**Responding to the Word**

**Sharing in the Eucharist brings us into greater communion, both with God and with others. What can I do to show my unity with others when I participate in the Eucharist?**

_____

_____

_____

_____

_____

_____

_____

_____

_____

_____

_____

_____

_____

_____

_____

_____

_____

_____

_____

_____

_____

_____

_____

_____

## Final Thoughts ...

_____

_____

_____

_____

## Feasts this Week

**June 13    St Anthony of Padua**
**June 16    The Most Sacred Heart of Jesus**
**June 17    The Immaculate Heart of the Blessed Virgin Mary**

# 11th Sunday in Ordinary Time

IT'S WONDERFUL TO observe the father of a newborn child. A deeply rooted instinct rises to the surface as he hovers over his wife and infant. He will do anything to protect them and to provide for their security and well-being. It's equally wonderful to hear stories at the funeral vigil of a faithful husband and father as stories are told by family and friends about camping trips, soccer games, dancing lessons, and part-time jobs to make ends meet. Jesus' choice to call God *Abba*, the equivalent of *Dad*, speaks volumes about his relationship with Joseph who, in his own human experience of intimacy and tenderness, provided him with his favorite image for the Almighty.

The Scriptures today present images of tenderness and care that reflect the best instincts of fathers and mothers alike. The poetry of the Bible suggests that "eagles' wings" – eagles sometimes bear their young aloft and at other times protect them under their shadow – is a metaphor for God's way of caring for his beloved children. The nurturing and protective responsibilities of a shepherd that Jesus uses to describe his own ministry provide yet another image of God's way of gathering and keeping a family together. Both of these rich and evocative images of God invite emulation by mothers and fathers, pastors and teachers, and anyone else who shares responsibility for the welfare of human beings and communities.

*Rev. Corbin Eddy*

---

**People and Prayers to Remember this Week**

_____

_____

_____

---

*Readings of the Day* ─────────────────────────

Exodus 19.1-6a               Romans 5.6-11
Psalm 100                    Matthew 9.36 – 10.8

**Responding to the Word**

**The people of the covenant are to be God's "special possession." How can I thank God for being included in the new covenant people?**

_____

_____

_____

_____

_____

_____

_____

_____

_____

## Final Thoughts ...

## Feasts this Week

June 19   **St Romuald**
June 21   **St Aloysius Gonzaga**
June 22   **St Paulinus of Nola**
         **St John Fisher & St Thomas More**
June 24   **The Nativity of St John the Baptist**

# 12th Sunday in Ordinary Time

WHAT WE HEAR in the dark, we are to tell in the light. What is whispered in our ears is to be proclaimed from the rooftops. For disciples of Christ, then and now, hearing the gospel message carries a responsibility. Like Jeremiah and Jesus, we are responsible for speaking truth to a mostly deaf and disbelieving world.

Words of truth are rarely welcome. To speak of peace in a time of war is to risk rejection. To speak of mercy and forgiveness in the aftermath of violence is seen as soft-headed and simplistic. To speak of justice for all in the face of global inequality and exploitation is to invite persecution. As Jeremiah knew, and as disciples of Jesus discover, to be a truth-teller to the powers that be is an occupation fraught with difficulty and even danger. At best, one might be considered a laughingstock; at worst, one faces death.

As a Eucharistic people, gathered to hear and spread the Word, we too can be worried about the reactions we might receive. In the face of such worry, Jesus speaks directly: "Have no fear." As disciples we stand with Jesus, entrusting ourselves to him. Jesus reassures us of our value in God's eyes and we give thanks for the protection of the one who, holding even the birds of the air in a loving embrace, holds us ever closer.

*Sandy Prather*

**People and Prayers to Remember this Week**

_____

_____

_____

*Readings of the Day* ────────────────────

Jeremiah 20.10-13                 Romans 5.12-15
Psalm 69                          Matthew 10.26-33

**Responding to the Word**

**Jeremiah knows that God is with him in his troubles. What gives you confidence God is with you in times of trouble?**

_____

_____

_____

_____

_____

_____

_____

_____

_____

_____

_____

_____

_____

_____

_____

_____

_____

_____

_____

_____

_____

## Final Thoughts ...

_____

_____

_____

_____

## Feasts this Week

| | |
|---|---|
| **June 27** | **St Cyril of Alexandria** |
| | **Bl Nykyta Budka & Bl Vasyl Velychkowsky (Canada)** |
| **June 28** | **St Irenaeus** |
| **June 29** | **St Peter & St Paul** |
| **June 30** | **First Martyrs of the Holy Roman Church** |
| **July 1** | **St Junípero Serra (USA)** |
| | **Canada Day (Canada)** |

# 13th Sunday in Ordinary Time

WE ARE INVITED this week to reflect once more on the call and meaning of discipleship. Our discipleship is rooted in baptism in the death and resurrection of Jesus Christ. The reading from 2 Kings and our gospel today make concrete a demand of discipleship: namely, hospitality.

Traveling recently, I found myself surrounded by cultures that seemed strange and languages in which I wasn't very fluent. I continue to be grateful for those who offered me hospitality, orienting me to the culture of those around me, introducing me to new friends and colleagues, helping me to understand and be understood.

The unnamed woman of the first reading offers the passerby a meal. She later recognizes Elisha as a holy man and again provides him with a space to rest and a meal. Who are the unsung or even unnamed people in my life? Might I offer a prayer or a gesture or a blessing to those persons? Who are the passersby God might be inviting us to welcome? In the gospel, Jesus calls each of us to be rooted in him. We are urged to love and welcome others, to offer even a cup of water, as a disciple of Jesus, recognizing Christ in the family member and in the stranger.

We give thanks and praise today for God's goodness and steadfast love. We pledge ourselves to be women and men, children and youth of gospel hospitality. In this way we live the call to be disciples of Jesus.

*Sr. Carmen Diston, IBVM*

**People and Prayers to Remember this Week**

_Readings of the Day_ ─────────────────

2 Kings 4.8-12a, 14-16          Romans 6.3-4, 8-11
Psalm 89                        Matthew 10.37-42

**Responding to the Word**

**Paul talks about dying to sin and living for God. Which sin do I struggle with most that keeps me captive?**

_____

_____

_____

_____

_____

_____

_____

_____

_____

_____

_____

_____

_____

## Final Thoughts ...

_____

_____

_____

_____

## Feasts this Week

**July 3**   **St Thomas**
**July 4**   **St Elizabeth of Portugal (Canada)**
          **Independence Day (USA)**
**July 5**   **St Anthony Zaccaria**
          **St Elizabeth of Portugal (USA)**
**July 6**   **St Maria Goretti**

# 14th Sunday in Ordinary Time

PAUSE FOR A minute. Make a mental list of the different burdens that you (and the people you know) carry each day. Don't rush... give yourself time to really think about this.

Burdens come in all shapes and sizes, and most of us carry a few. Burdens can be small but annoying things that are eventually resolved by personal effort or some change in circumstance. They can be big, all-consuming issues that drag on for years and leave scars on our emotional or financial well-being. Burdens can also be on-going, systemic challenges due to poverty or illness or discrimination – situations that can't be altered without significant social change. In any event, carrying a burden – big or small, everyday or unusual – has a tremendous effect on our personal well-being and how we relate to each other.

Today's gospel reminds us that a faithful, reflective life can ease whatever load we carry. But it also presents a challenge to us. If putting our faith in Jesus is important, then as followers of Jesus, we have a responsibility to connect with the people around us, to get to know the burdens that they are carrying, and to find ways to ease their load in whatever way we can. While each of us finds support in God, we also need to demonstrate our faith by supporting others. It is the gentle, humble-hearted thing to do.

*Susan Eaton*

**People and Prayers to Remember this Week**

_Readings of the Day_

Zechariah 9.9-10               Romans 8.9, 11-13
Psalm 145                      Matthew 11.25-30

**Responding to the Word**

**The messianic king is a gentle ruler who brings peace. When have you experienced the peace of Jesus?**

_____

_____

_____

_____

_____

_____

_____

_____

_____

_____

_____

_____

## Final Thoughts ...

_____

_____

_____

_____

## Feasts this Week

**July 11    St Benedict**

**July 13    St Henry**

**July 14    St Camillus de Lellis (Canada)**
**St Kateri Tekakwitha (USA)**

**July 15    St Bonaventure**

# 15th Sunday in Ordinary Time

TODAY, THE WORD of God is compared to seed, the source that goes out to bring forth new life. All of our life, all of creation, is groaning in anticipation of being all we can become. Every springtime, when working in my back yard, I'm not completely sure of the hue of the flowers from the seed I'm planting, nor do I exactly know the taste of the tomatoes. I do know that I must prepare the soil, fertilize, weed, and water. By the same token, we have to activate the seed of faith we've been given, and care for it, in order to see it grow. The passage in Matthew's gospel for next Sunday promises that a massive mustard tree can grow from even the tiniest of seeds.

If we allow ourselves to become like the Pharisees, however, the opportunity for God's grace to really touch our hearts is about as likely as the chance for seed to grow on paths, on rocky ground, or among thorns. With very firm language, Jesus continually warns his followers against refusing to value the Word of God and to act upon it after they have received it.

Rather, when we cultivate the hearts of disciples, we can listen and hear the Word. We can respond as does a fertile field, allowing the source of life to grow within us.

How might we encourage our faith to grow?

*Joe Gunn*

**People and Prayers to Remember this Week**

_Readings of the Day_

Isaiah 55.10-11                    Romans 8.18-23
Psalm 65                          Matthew 13.1-23

**Responding to the Word**

**God's word changes our world. What changes have I experienced due to my attention to Scripture?**

_____

_____

_____

_____

_____

_____

_____

_____

_____

_____

_____

_____

_____

_____

## Final Thoughts ...

_____

_____

_____

_____

## Feasts this Week

**July 18    St Camillus de Lellis (USA)**
**July 20    St Apollinaris**
**July 21    St Lawrence of Brindisi**
**July 22    St Mary Magdalene**

# 16th Sunday in Ordinary Time

I REMEMBER THE first time I saw her. Long nails, flashy jewelry, dyed hair, and dressed to kill. "Shallow," whispered that judgmental little voice in my brain. Who would ever have imagined that she would turn out to be one of the deepest, most spiritual people I know.

How easy it is for us to judge others, only to find out later how wrong we really were. That's exactly what Jesus is trying to get across to us today with the parable of the weeds and the wheat. At first glance, it seems to make no sense. What farmer wants weeds to take over his crop? But if we dig a little deeper, we see that's not the point Jesus is trying to make. He's not denying that the weeds are there, or saying that they don't need to be separated from the wheat. What he is saying is that it's not up to us to do the weeding. Only God can separate the weeds from the wheat, the bad from the good.

Instead of trying to be the one doing the weeding, perhaps we should try a little harder to be the wheat. Instead of judging who is good and holy and who is not, we could try to *be* good and holy and leave it at that. For my part, I'm glad the rest is up to God.

*Teresa Whalen Lux*

**People and Prayers to Remember this Week**

*Readings of the Day* ———————————————

Wisdom 12.13, 16-19                    Romans 8.26-27
Psalm 86                               Matthew 13.24-43

**Responding to the Word**

**The Holy Spirit helps us to pray when we don't know how.
For what help with my prayer do I ask the Holy Spirit today?**

_____

_____

_____

_____

_____

_____

_____

_____

_____

_____

_____

_____

_____

_____

## Final Thoughts ...

_____

_____

_____

## Feasts this Week

**July 24   St Sharbel Makhlūf**
**July 25   St James**
**July 26   St Anne & St Joachim**
**July 29   St Martha, St Mary & St Lazarus**

# *17th Sunday in Ordinary Time*

WHILE TODAY'S GOSPEL presents us with images of the kingdom, reading between the lines we see that the focus of the parables isn't hidden treasure, pearls, or fish. It is the actions of the hunter, the merchant, and the fishermen.

What does the gospel tell us about these people? The treasure hunter, the merchant, and the fishermen are relentless in their search for the prize. They are persistent in the face of challenges and they become innovative in looking for ways to overcome the obstacles they face. At times these people may be very much "in your face" and hence not appreciated by others.

If we are going to build the kingdom, we, like the treasure hunter, the merchant, and the fishermen, must be relentless. We are called to face obstacles and we are called to be innovative in the ways in which we overcome these challenges. Our culture may not appreciate our persistence. Our actions may be seen as "in your face" – but building the kingdom requires action and behavior which some may consider extreme.

To be persistent, to work to overcome challenges in an innovative manner, to be extreme without being a fanatic – this is our call, in union with the source of our strength, the Eucharist. The Eucharist gives faith to dispel fear, hope to build confidence, and love to serve as Jesus did.

*Anthony Chezzi*

**People and Prayers to Remember this Week**

_Readings of the Day_

1 Kings 3.5-12          Romans 8.28-30
Psalm 119              Matthew 13.44-52

**Responding to the Word**

**Solomon asks God for an understanding heart. What would I ask God for?**

_____

_____

_____

_____

_____

_____

_____

_____

_____

_____

_____

## Final Thoughts …

_____

_____

_____

_____

## Feasts this Week

| July 31 | **St Ignatius of Loyola** |
|---------|---------------------------|
| August 1 | **St Alphonsus Liguori** |
| August 2 | **St Eusebius of Vercelli** |
| | **St Peter Julian Eymard** |
| August 4 | **St John Mary Vianney** |
| August 5 | **Dedication of the Basilica of St Mary Major** |
| | **Bl Frédéric Janssoone (Canada)** |

# *Transfiguration of the Lord*

TODAY'S READINGS ERUPT with images of a God whose immensity is beyond our understanding. They take us from Daniel's dream vision of a fiery "Ancient One," to the psalm's evocation of God's all-encompassing power, to the disciples' mountaintop experience of the transfigured Jesus bathed in light and flanked by the prophets. It is little wonder that Peter, James, and John cower in fear at the voice of this terrifying and overwhelming God!

How can we dare to even think about, let alone approach, such awesome immensity? For Christians, the answer is found in Jesus himself. See what happens next in the Transfiguration scene. What does Jesus do when the three disciples fall to the ground in terror? Bending down to touch them, he says the words that he repeats so often in the gospel narratives: "Do not be afraid." And after the swirling maelstrom of light and sound and heart-stopping majesty, suddenly they see only "Jesus himself alone."

To echo Peter's words in his eyewitness account of the gospel event, we would "do well to be attentive to this as to a lamp shining in a dark place." The transcendent God who is beyond our wildest imaginings is the same God who tenderly invites each of us into an intimate relationship of love. This is a profound mystery and a priceless gift.

*Krystyna Higgins*

**People and Prayers to Remember this Week**

_____

_____

_____

*Readings of the Day* ───────────────────────────

Daniel 7.9-10, 13-14                 2 Peter 1.16-19
Psalm 97                             Matthew 17.1-9

**Responding to the Word**

When the disciples hear the voice of God, they fall to the
ground in fear. When has my experiencing God's presence
led me to be fearful. Why?

_____

_____

_____

_____

_____

_____

_____

_____

_____

## Final Thoughts ...

## Feasts this Week

| | |
|---|---|
| **August 7** | **St Sixtus II & Companions** |
| | **St Cajetan** |
| **August 8** | **St Dominic** |
| **August 9** | **St Teresa Benedicta of the Cross** |
| **August 10** | **St Lawrence** |
| **August 11** | **St Clare** |
| **August 12** | **St Jane Frances de Chantal** |

# *19th Sunday in Ordinary Time*

SUMMER IS THE time when most people stop to rest, relax, and enjoy the long days and warm sunshine. Life abounds and we drink it in, storing up energy and memories for times when sunshine and flowers seem far away.

Today's gospel and first reading reflect a situation not unlike our summer experience. In the gospel, Jesus leaves behind the busyness of life to withdraw and spend some time alone in quiet prayer. He had just preached to the crowds and fed them and now, knowing that he needs to be fed himself, he goes to the mountain to be alone with God.

Elijah's story is quite different. Discouraged by the fact that his work for God was not accepted, Elijah has no desire to continue living. But he goes to the mountain of God where, in silence, he waits for God to meet him. And God does come, although it is not in the way Elijah expects. God touches him in the quiet stillness of a gentle breeze and gives him courage to continue his mission.

Like Elijah and Jesus we need to find the time and space to have a "summer moment" with God. Today's readings are an invitation to enter the silence, be touched by the gentle breeze, and become aware of God's presence in ordinary moments – in the beauty of nature, in the love of a friend, in our Eucharistic celebration.

*Sr. Barbara A. Bozak, CSJ*

**People and Prayers to Remember this Week**

_Readings of the Day_

1 Kings 19.9, 11-13　　　　　Romans 9.1-5
Psalm 85　　　　　　　　　Matthew 14.22-33

**Responding to the Word**

**Elijah hears God only in the faint, whispering sound. What tiny whispers from God have I noticed recently?**

## Final Thoughts ...

## Feasts this Week

August 14    **St Maximilian Kolbe**
August 15    **The Assumption of the Blessed Virgin Mary**
August 16    **St Stephen of Hungary**
August 19    **St John Eudes**

# *Assumption of the Blessed Virgin Mary*

MARY'S PRAYER IN today's gospel passage is both humble and confident. Following her cousin Elizabeth's proclamation of Mary as blessed among women, Mary replies with her hymn of praise to God: her Magnificat.

Mary says, "My soul magnifies the Lord" and firmly sets her confidence in God. Though birthing God for the world must have seemed utterly impossible to Mary, she trusts that God will fulfill his plans with her. Her ongoing faith-filled response to God's call, uniquely miraculous and difficult as it is, should inspire us to trust in God with such radical confidence ourselves – not a confidence that overinflates our sense of self, elevating ourselves above others, but one that is rooted in God's care and mercy. This value on humble confidence is echoed later: God "has brought down the powerful... and lifted up the lowly." Though Jesus has not yet been born, Mary recognizes that God is already present in the midst of his people in a new way in her pregnant body, to which John responds with joy while still in Elizabeth's womb.

Mary carries Jesus in her womb; we carry him with our lives. May we see that God invites us to embrace the humble confidence of Mary in our own lives, recognizing that God is already at work in us to bring mercy into the world.

*Kelly Bourke*

**People and Prayers to Remember this Week**

*Readings of the Day* —————————————————

Revelation 11.19a; 12.1-6, 10ab    1 Corinthians 15.20-27
Psalm 45                           Luke 1.39-56

**Responding to the Word**

Mary's song of praise speaks of God lifting up the lowly. Where have I seen God bring about justice in an unjust situation?

**Final Thoughts ...**

# 20th Sunday in Ordinary Time

TODAY'S GOSPEL ABOUT the woman from Canaan is a demonstration of God's kindness. It also highlights the virtues of faith, humility, and perseverance. When Jesus did not heed her request the first time, and his disciples urged him to ignore her, the Canaanite woman fell to her knees and humbled herself before him. Moved by her faith, Jesus cured her daughter. There was something about her faith and humility and her unwillingness to get discouraged that impressed Jesus. She believed in him, and she came out of that encounter refreshed and renewed.

Jesus' mercy and justice shine through in this encounter. We can imitate his example and open our hearts to all people, no matter where they come from, no matter what the difficulties are. For it is only through this openness of spirit that we communicate and share with everyone the essence of God's love. Rev. Richard Humke, an Episcopalian priest, has noted: "In the context of the Lord's supper, where we all come knowing that none of us is perfect and that each of us has failed... something good happens in our life as a community when we notice the people around us." Jesus noticed the woman from Canaan for her faith. "Woman, great is your faith!" Jesus invites us to open our hearts and believe.

*Sharon Queano*

**People and Prayers to Remember this Week**

*Readings of the Day* ─────────────────────────

Isaiah 56.1, 6-7                    Romans 11.13-15, 29-32
Psalm 67                           Matthew 15.21-28

**Responding to the Word**

Isaiah reminds us that God wants the temple to be a house of prayer for all persons. What can I do to make my household more prayerful?

_____

_____

_____

_____

_____

_____

_____

_____

_____

_____

_____

_____

## Final Thoughts ...

_____

_____

_____

_____

## Feasts this Week

| | |
|---|---|
| **August 21** | **St Pius X** |
| **August 22** | **The Queenship of the Blessed Virgin Mary** |
| **August 23** | **St Rose of Lima** |
| **August 24** | **St Bartholomew** |
| **August 25** | **St Louis** |
| | **St Joseph Calasanz** |

# 21st Sunday in Ordinary Time

How OFTEN HAVE we heard the old adage: practice makes perfect. It drove me crazy when Mom would say it as I practiced my piano scales yet again. But Peter's declaration of faith in today's gospel is a good case in point of just how true that saying really is. Throughout the gospels, we see the many times Peter tried to practice his faith in Jesus. Attempting to walk on water – and sinking! Or swearing that he will stand by Jesus – and then denying him!

And yet, today's gospel is a shining example of a time when Peter *did* get it right, when all of his practice finally paid off. Out of all Jesus' followers, Peter is the one whose faith allows him to be the first to proclaim that Jesus is the Messiah.

Each week when we come together to celebrate the Eucharist, we, too, profess our faith in Jesus as God's only Son, *our* Lord. And each week we are sent forth to practice – and to put *into* practice – what we have proclaimed. When we refuse to hold on to hurts or grudges and offer forgiveness to another, when we welcome the newly arrived refugee next door, when we act with compassion to the less fortunate, we practice what we have proclaimed.

"Who do you say that I am?" Today, we go forth to live out the answer in the world.

*Teresa Whalen Lux*

**People and Prayers to Remember this Week**

_____

_____

_____

*Readings of the Day* ——————————————

Isaiah 22.15, 19-23                    Romans 11.33-36
Psalm 138                              Matthew 16.13-20

**Responding to the Word**

**God's doorkeeper must not abuse his authority but care for those under his authority. How might I care more for those under my authority?**

_____

_____

_____

_____

_____

_____

_____

_____

_____

_____

_____

_____

_____

_____

_____

_____

_____

_____

_____

_____

_____

_____

_____

_____

_____

_____

## Final Thoughts ...

_____

_____

_____

_____

## Feasts this Week

**August 28     St Augustine**
**August 29     The Passion of St John the Baptist**

# 22nd Sunday in Ordinary Time

SHE SAT IN the recliner, pillows supporting her head. After the operation she had decided against chemotherapy. "Are you afraid?" I asked. She nodded emphatically. In that moment I knew the depths of her trust. Years ago she had said "Yes" to Jesus, and now he walked her gently through the valley of death.

Peter does not grasp that Jesus is fully human, and that his messiahship commits him to human suffering. Jesus exhorts his disciples, and us, to take up the cross and follow him. That is the key: walking our path with Jesus through loss, or failure, or illness, and finding a deeper, more joy-filled life. As we walk with Jesus, we become more fully human.

My friend, a fellow member of my religious community, had known opposition in taking a stand for the rights of those in need. As I sat next to her at morning Eucharist, being present to Jesus' suffering, death, and resurrection, I recalled how she had taught me the ways of God. The whole world is no exchange for the life Jesus offers.

Today at Eucharist we hear again Jesus taking up the cross. "This is my body which will be given up for you; this is the cup of my blood." And we give thanks that he walks with us on the wondrous journey of life.

*Sr. Linda Hayward, RSCJ*

**People and Prayers to Remember this Week**

_Readings of the Day_ —————————————

Jeremiah 20.7-9                     Romans 12.1-2
Psalm 63                           Matthew 16.21-27

**Responding to the Word**

**Paul encourages us to be transformed so we know what is good and pleasing to God. What do I most need to change in my life to be more pleasing to God?**

_____

_____

_____

_____

_____

_____

_____

_____

_____

_____

_____

_____

_____

_____

_____

**Final Thoughts ...**

_____

_____

_____

_____

**Feasts this Week**

| | |
|---|---|
| **September 4** | **Bl Dina Bélanger (Canada)** |
| **September 8** | **The Nativity of the Blessed Virgin Mary** |
| **September 9** | **St Peter Claver** |

# 23rd Sunday in Ordinary Time

IN TODAY'S FIRST reading, Ezekiel receives a command: warn Israel to turn away from its current, perilous lifestyle. It is a matter of life or death for both prophet and people, lest they sleepwalk into captivity and exile. Underlying this stark warning is the intense passion of God for their well-being, and God's invitation to return again to safety through obedience to the voice of their shepherd.

How we hate to be reprimanded for wrongdoing. In the gospel today, Jesus teaches us how to help each other overcome the hurt caused by our sinfulness. Correction of a community member is to be done lovingly and with care. In this manner, the offender is restored to wholeness as a person; they can then live fully and freely in relationship to God and others.

What happens on a personal level can lead, on a larger scale, to the healing of communities and nations. Ezekiel's mission could equally be applied to our world today and the painful condition of whole nations – indeed, of creation itself. God's passion is for all peoples to live in peace, dignity, and freedom, and for the gifts of creation to be respected and shared fairly. We are charged by Christ to do all that we can to restore life and promote healing among ourselves and for creation. As Christians, we are, by vocation, healers and reconcilers to the world around us.

*Rev. Michael Traher, SFM*

**People and Prayers to Remember this Week**

_____

_____

_____

*Readings of the Day* ───────────────────

**Ezekiel 33.7-9**          **Romans 13.8-10**
**Psalm 95**                **Matthew 18.15-20**

**Responding to the Word**

**Jesus encourages us to find a practical way toward reconciliation. With whom might I need to reconcile today?**

_____

_____

_____

_____

_____

_____

_____

_____

_____

_____

_____

_____

_____

_____

_____

_____

_____

_____

_____

_____

_____

_____

## Final Thoughts ...

_____

_____

_____

_____

## Feasts this Week

| | |
|---|---|
| September 12 | **The Most Holy Name of Mary** |
| September 13 | **St John Chrysostom** |
| September 14 | **The Exaltation of the Holy Cross** |
| September 15 | **Our Lady of Sorrows** |
| September 16 | **St Cornelius & St Cyprian** |

# 24th Sunday in Ordinary Time

WHAT A PUZZLE a human being is! Take that slave in today's gospel passage. His debt was enormous. The king was entitled to balance his books by selling the slave, his few possessions, and even his wife and children – possibly to different owners. But the slave asked for patience on the part of the king and was granted mercy in abundance. The king erased his entire debt! This was beyond what the slave had hoped or asked for. His money problems were gone in an instant.

You'd think this slave would be overflowing with "the milk of human kindness." But no! He had his neighbor thrown into debtors' prison. Truly, this slave's behavior does not make sense. Sin seldom makes sense. We're led to ask, "What were you thinking?!" When we take time to reflect on our own bad acts, we realize that we should have known better; we do know better. This is the mystery of sin.

The king's behavior doesn't make sense either. Who in their right mind would simply erase such a large debt? Who could be so gracious? Who but God, the true king! God's grace is also a mystery. As we leave the liturgy today, we are sent forth in the peace of Christ, carrying within us God's mercy and forgiveness which are meant to be passed on to those we meet this week.

*Margaret Bick*

**People and Prayers to Remember this Week**

_____

_____

_____

*Readings of the Day* ———————————————————————

Sirach 27.30 – 28.7          Romans 14.7-9
Psalm 103                    Matthew 18.21-35

**Responding to the Word**

**The people looked on the bronze serpent for God's healing.
What has been a source of healing for me?**

_____

_____

_____

_____

_____

_____

_____

_____

_____

_____

## Final Thoughts ...

## Feasts this Week

# 25th Sunday in Ordinary Time

TODAY'S GOSPEL, THE parable of the landowner and the laborers, begins with negotiation and recruiting, and ends with payday. I couldn't find a middle. What fruitful labor are the workers called to and paid for? What do they accomplish? It is as if the landowner calls the workers unconditionally, saying, "Come on in. I will pay you a just wage. You have nothing better to do, so let's see what happens under these conditions."

And what conditions they are! Negotiations begin. The usual daily wage is established. Flexible hours are encouraged. Idle workers are recruited. Grumbling is not allowed. The employer is generous.

What an opportunity! Perhaps there is no middle to this parable because these conditions rarely exist in the real world. Today 20 per cent of the world's population consumes more than 80 per cent of the earth's resources. One billion people go to bed hungry every night. Such an imbalance could not exist in the vineyard of today's gospel.

We are invited to be like the landowner: flexible, fair, generous. We can "fill in the blanks" of this parable with justice for workers and an equitable distribution of God's earthly gifts.

*John Weir*

**People and Prayers to Remember this Week**

_____

_____

_____

*Readings of the Day* ───────────────────────

Isaiah 55.6-9                    Philippians 1.20-24, 27
Psalm 145                       Matthew 20.1-16

**Responding to the Word**

**Paul encourages us to conduct ourselves in a way worthy of the gospel. What can I do today to offer an example of gospel living?**

_____

_____

_____

_____

_____

_____

_____

_____

_____

_____

_____

_____

_____

_____

_____

_____

_____

_____

_____

_____

## Final Thoughts ...

_____

_____

_____

_____

## Feasts this Week

| | |
|---|---|
| **September 26** | **St John de Brébeuf, St Isaac Jogues & Companions (Canada)** |
| | **St Cosmas & St Damian (USA)** |
| **September 27** | **St Vincent de Paul** |
| **September 28** | **St Wenceslaus** |
| | **St Lawrence Riuz & Companions** |
| **September 29** | **St Michael, St Gabriel & St Raphael** |
| **September 30** | **St Jerome** |

# 26th Sunday in Ordinary Time

AT A RECENT meeting we were naming the personal qualities we were looking for in a search to fill an important position. The first quality mentioned was "follow-through... she has to have follow-through." All of us appreciate those people who actually do what they say they are going to do. We can trust them and depend on them.

In today's gospel Jesus describes two kinds of people – those who say "no" at first but then do it anyhow, and those who say "yes" and don't follow through. In the end, it is those who do God's will who will be judged as righteous. Jesus reminds us that we might be surprised at those we meet in the reign of God. Tax collectors and prostitutes don't seem like likely candidates. What about drug dealers and crooked politicians in our day? How do they line up against the more religious, law-abiding citizens?

As we celebrate the Eucharist, we are a gathering of all kinds of people who are here for all kinds of reasons. It is not for us to judge each other's motivation. What is essential is that all of us are embraced by the unconditional love and mercy of God and by the magnanimity of Jesus whose eternal "yes" liberates us to live in the Spirit.

*Sr. Mary Ellen Green, OP*

## People and Prayers to Remember this Week

_Readings of the Day_ ———————————————

Ezekiel 18.25-28                    Philippians 2.1-11
Psalm 25                            Matthew 21.28-32

**Responding to the Word**

**Paul offers ways that we can improve our relationships
with others. Which of his suggestions might I do today?**

## Final Thoughts …

## Feasts this Week

| | |
|---|---|
| **October 2** | **The Holy Guardian Angels** |
| **October 4** | **St Francis of Assisi** |
| **October 5** | **St Faustina Kowalska** |
| | **Bl Francis Xavier Seelos (USA)** |
| **October 6** | **Bl Marie-Rose Durocher** |
| | **St Bruno** |
| **October 7** | **Our Lady of the Rosary** |

# *27th Sunday in Ordinary Time*

EVERYBODY KNOWS SOMEONE who thinks the world owes them a living. Psychologists call this having a sense of entitlement. A sense of entitlement dulls, or even kills, a person's ability to feel thankful. If I deserve everything I get (or want), there is no room for gratitude.

The plants in the vineyard, the tenants in Jesus' story, and the authorities in Jerusalem seem to have suffered from a sense of entitlement. The ungrateful vines produced sour grapes. The tenants failed to recognize their interdependent partnership with the landlord. The Jerusalem authorities saw their social status as a sign of God's approval, a sign of their salvation. The problem is not that they failed to "earn their keep"; it's that their sense of entitlement hobbled their ability to respond with gratitude to what they had received.

The weekly Sunday Eucharist trains us in this attitude. As the Greek name indicates (*eucharistia* = thanksgiving), thanksgiving is at the heart of our Sunday gathering. At the beginning of every Eucharistic prayer at every Mass we declare, "It is truly right and just... to give [God] thanks." This prayer is the Church's great prayer of thanks at the banquet table of the Lord. What prayers of thanksgiving do you bring along to Mass today? What fruits do your gifts call you to bring forth to the world?

*Margaret Bick*

**People and Prayers to Remember this Week**

_____

_____

_____

*Readings of the Day* ——————————————————————

Isaiah 5.1-7                         Philippians 4.6-9
Psalm 80                             Matthew 21.33-43

**Responding to the Word**

**God tends to us like a vineyard owner working to make sure
that he will have a good crop. How have I experienced God's
workings in me recently?**

_____

_____

_____

_____

_____

_____

_____

_____

_____

_____

_____

_____

_____

_____

_____

_____

_____

_____

_____

_____

_____

_____

## Final Thoughts …

_____

_____

_____

_____

## Feasts this Week

| | |
|---|---|
| **October 9** | **St Denis & Companions** |
| | **St John Leonardi** |
| | **Thanksgiving Day (Canada)** |
| **October 11** | **St John XXIII** |
| **October 14** | **St Callistus I** |

# 28th Sunday in Ordinary Time

"GO THEREFORE INTO the main streets, and invite everyone you find to the wedding banquet." These words of Jesus express our prime vocation and our greatest challenge as Christians. We may lament the decrease in numbers in church attendance and the scarce exposure given by the media to religious issues. But it still remains our responsibility to "go out into the main streets," to reach out to people whoever and wherever they are. Why? To let them know that our God has no other plan for humankind than gathering all peoples together for a banquet, a wedding feast of unmatched magnitude and duration.

"The main streets" of today's world swarm with people hustling and bustling for work, business, shopping, and entertainment. They also abound in people who are jobless, homeless, feeling helpless. The former might have no time even to consider God's invitation to his banquet, and the latter may feel that God ignores their needs and aspirations. Rich or poor, good or bad, they are all in dire need of hearing and experiencing some good news.

In today's Eucharist, may we realize the richness of God's banquet and his deepest desire to see the banquet hall "filled with guests." May we also, in the coming days and weeks, "go into the streets" and share the good news of a munificent God inviting everyone to join the banquet he has prepared for all people.

*Jean-Pierre Prévost*

---

**People and Prayers to Remember this Week**

_____

_____

_____

---

*Readings of the Day* ————————————————

Isaiah 25.6-10a                    Philippians 4.12-14, 19-20
Psalm 23                           Matthew 22.1-14

**Responding to the Word**

**God invites us to the banquet, but we must be responsible for how we act. What can I do today to be more generous in my response to God's call?**

_____

_____

_____

_____

_____

_____

_____

_____

_____

_____

_____

_____

_____

_____

_____

_____

_____

## Final Thoughts …

_____

_____

_____

_____

## Feasts this Week

| | |
|---|---|
| **October 16** | **St Marguerite d'Youville (Canada)** |
| | **St Hedwig (USA)** |
| | **St Margaret Mary Alacoque (USA)** |
| **October 17** | **St Ignatius of Antioch** |
| **October 18** | **St Luke** |
| **October 19** | **St John de Brébeuf, St Isaac Jogues & Companions (USA)** |
| | **St Paul of the Cross (Canada)** |
| **October 20** | **St Hedwig (Canada)** |
| | **St Margaret Mary Alacoque (Canada)** |
| | **St Paul of the Cross (USA)** |

# 29th Sunday in Ordinary Time

WHILE I HAVE heard and read this gospel many times over the years, in the past I failed to fully understand the principle that Jesus demonstrates to the Pharisees and the Herodians as well as us today.

Jesus was very aware that the question asked was a trick question. Had he answered, "Don't pay taxes or give to the Temple," then either his followers would have reason to mistrust him or the Pharisees and Herodians would report him to the authorities. Jesus was asked to decide the legality of paying taxes. His answer, "Give therefore to the emperor the things that are the emperor's and to God the things that are God's," places the responsibility for discernment on the person making the decision.

Today we are called to balance our lives between the morality of our faith and the morality of the secular world. Do we go to Mass on Sunday or do we go to the football game? Do we make time to visit the sick and serve others or are we occupied with self-serving activities? Through prayer, faith, and following the principles of Jesus, we are guided to discern the right choices. Though we live in the secular world and have responsibilities as well as rights in that world, we must be conscious of the rights and responsibilities we have in our faith and in our calling.

*Susan Berlingeri*

**People and Prayers to Remember this Week**

_____

_____

_____

*Readings of the Day* ─────────────────────────

Isaiah 45.1, 4-6                    1 Thessalonians 1.1-5ab
Psalm 96                            Matthew 22.15-21

**Responding to the Word**

**God governs political events even though political rulers do
not know it. Where do I detect God's presence in political
events today?**

_____

_____

_____

_____

_____

_____

_____

_____

_____

_____

_____

_____

_____

_____

_____

_____

_____

_____

_____

_____

_____

_____

_____

_____

_____

## Final Thoughts ...

_____

_____

_____

_____

## Feasts this Week

**October 23**   **St John of Capistrano**

**October 24**   **St Anthony Mary Claret**

**October 28**   **St Simon & St Jude**

# 30th Sunday in Ordinary Time

THERE IS A beautiful Norwegian folk tale that says before a soul is united with a body, the soul is kissed by God. During its life on earth, the soul holds a powerful memory of that kiss. This is the background music for a lifetime. My lifelong task is to see that God's original kiss lives on in my words and actions that heal, support, and forgive others.

In answering the lawyer's question about the greatest commandment, Jesus responds from his lived experience of a loving intimate relationship with God. It sounds so simple – just love God and love your neighbor. Jesus, however, showed just how challenging this is. Love led him to reach out to the outcasts of his day and, in so doing, he experienced the disapproval and rejection of many. In a simple gesture toward the end of his life, Jesus took a basin of water and began to wash feet, asking those who believed in him to do the same.

The two commandments of love have not changed. The challenge to live them remains just as daunting today as in the time of Jesus. Can we love enough to forgive? Will we become peacemakers in our families, workplace, or community? In these questions lies the essence of Jesus' commandments. Yes, they require faith and action fueled by strength and determination. But we are strengthened by a kiss from God.

*Sr. Judy Morris, OP*

## People and Prayers to Remember this Week

_Readings of the Day_

Exodus 22.21-27 (Canada)          1 Thessalonians 1.5c-10
Exodus 22.20-26 (USA)             Matthew 22.34-40
Psalm 18

### Responding to the Word

**God's special compassion is for those most vulnerable who are liable to be victimized by others. What can I do to help someone who is vulnerable?**

Final Thoughts ...

## Feasts this Week

**November 1**   **All Saints**
**November 2**   **All Souls' Day**
**November 3**   **St Martin de Porres**
**November 4**   **St Charles Borromeo**

# *All Saints*

TODAY WE CELEBRATE and give thanks for the witness and companionship of those we call the saints. The communion of saints includes, in its broadest sense, not only those formally recognized by the Church but also the exemplary people of faith whom we encounter in our communities and our families. The saints – both those who have gone before us and those who walk among us still – are icons of holiness, windows through which we glimpse the face of God.

All of us are called to holiness, to a life shaped by gospel values. Today's reading of the Beatitudes offers us some guidelines. Bombarded by the lures of consumerism, we are called to be poor in spirit. In a world beset by war and violence, we are called to be peacemakers. In a society that prioritizes competitiveness and ruthless individuality, we are called to be humble. Where grief and discouragement prevail, we are called to be merciful. In the face of injustice, we are invited to "hunger and thirst for righteousness."

Today we pray for the grace to recognize that we are all called to be saints. In the words of the psalm, may we live with "clean hands and pure hearts," as we look forward in hope to sharing in the light of eternal life.

*Krystyna Higgins*

**People and Prayers to Remember this Week**

_Readings of the Day_

Revelation 7.2-4, 9-14          1 John 3.1-3
Psalm 24                        Matthew 5.1-12a

**Responding to the Word**

The Beatitudes tell us that we are blessed when people persecute us on God's account. When have I felt such persecution in my life?

**Final Thoughts ...**

# 31st Sunday in Ordinary Time

As AUTUMN MOVES to winter and the days get shorter, we seek ways to bring light into our lives. Everyone recognizes the contrast between the glow of one candle and complete darkness, for a single candle can make a difference in how and what we see.

In today's readings, we cannot fail to note the contrast between Paul's attitude in the second reading and that of the scribes and Pharisees of the gospel.

The scribes and Pharisees of whom Jesus speaks are focused entirely on themselves: how they might be honored and recognized. Yet they do nothing to earn this, but only lay burdens on the people. Their focus on themselves is in stark contrast to Paul's attitude toward the Thessalonians. Paul made no demands on the community. He was gentle with them and so reflected the light and warmth of God. We can imagine that the community responded not only to what Paul said but to how he lived, and so recognized Paul's words as the words of God.

These readings lead us to ponder our own lives, to see whether how we live reflects the attitude of the priests, scribes, and Pharisees or that of Paul. As Eucharistic people we, like Paul, are invited to proclaim, by the light and warmth of our lives, God's presence to all we meet.

*Sr. Barbara Bozak, CSJ*

**People and Prayers to Remember this Week**

_Readings of the Day_

Malachi 1.14 – 2.2, 8-10          1 Thessalonians 2.7-9, 13
Psalm 131                          Matthew 23.1-12

**Responding to the Word**

**Jesus reminds us to practice what we preach. Who in my life has been a good example of integrity in word and deed? What might I learn from them?**

**Final Thoughts ...**

**Feasts this Week**

| | |
|---|---|
| **November 9** | **The Dedication of the Lateran Basilica** |
| **November 10** | **St Leo the Great** |
| **November 11** | **St Martin of Tours** |

# 32nd Sunday in Ordinary Time

MOST PEOPLE HAVE had the experience at one time or another of preparing for a journey. It might have been preparing for a vacation; it might have been to visit relatives in other parts of the world. Whatever the reason, generally speaking it was interesting. Every human being is on a journey. For some the journey is short and perhaps colored with tragedy; for others it is a long life filled with periods of good times and bad times: but for all, it is a walk through life towards eternity.

In today's gospel, Matthew uses the example of two young women who acted differently in their preparation for meeting the bridegroom. One was completely ready, while the second one had yet to make a needed purchase and as a result she lost the opportunity to accompany the bridegroom when he arrived.

In this example we see the importance of not leaving details to the last minute. No doubt the lesson to be learned from this story of two young women is summed up in the words "Be Prepared." The whole gospel is directed to the need to be ready to meet the Lord when he calls us to leave this world and enter eternity. Since we have no way of knowing when we will be called to return to the Lord, Jesus warns us to be prepared at all times.

*Iris L. Kendall*

## People and Prayers to Remember this Week

_____

_____

_____

*Readings of the Day* ─────────────────────────

Wisdom 6.12-16                1 Thessalonians 4.13-18
Psalm 63                      Matthew 25.1-13

### Responding to the Word

**Wisdom is found by those who seek her. Where have I found wisdom in my life? Where do I look for wisdom?**

_____

_____

_____

_____

_____

_____

_____

_____

_____

_____

_____

_____

_____

_____

_____

_____

_____

_____

_____

_____

_____

## Final Thoughts ...

_____

_____

_____

_____

## Feasts this Week

| | |
|---|---|
| **November 13** | **St Frances Xavier Cabrini (USA)** |
| **November 15** | **St Albert the Great** |
| **November 16** | **St Margaret of Scotland** |
| | **St Gertrude** |
| **November 17** | **St Elizabeth of Hungary** |
| **November 18** | **Dedication of the Basilicas of St Peter & St Paul** |
| | **St Rose Philippine Duchesne (USA)** |

# *33rd Sunday in Ordinary Time*

WITHIN US IS a unique heart-song placed there by God. Our vocation is to respond to this gift by singing the song and leaving a voiceprint for others to hear. We might not be the first violin or the loudest trumpet, but without that one note from a simple triangle a symphony is incomplete.

We may think we are civilized, yet we are often confronted by evil wrought by human hands. This may be because we do not choose to develop our talents and so make the world a better place. Have we became tone-deaf to God's heart-song? Have we buried our talent? Gifts grow with use but wither with neglect. If we risk nothing, we gain nothing. If we risk even a little and deposit just one talent, eternal reward can be ours.

Whenever time runs out, we typically muse about what might have been and regret what we have squandered or wasted. As this liturgical year draws to a close, let us not rue the past. Instead, let us rediscover our heart-song and help others discover theirs. Let us reach out with the power of that song and sing it loud and clear. Then, let us listen for the voice of the Master calling us home: "Well done." Our vocation is to receive from God the gift of who we are and return that gift to God through an authentic response.

*Wanda Conway*

**People and Prayers to Remember this Week**

_____

_____

_____

*Readings of the Day* ————————————————————

Proverbs 31.10-13, 16-18, 20, 26, 28-31
Psalm 128

1 Thessalonians 5.1-6
Matthew 25.14-30

**Responding to the Word**

**In Jesus' parable, the servants are accountable for the talents they are given. How am I using the talents that God has given me?**

_____

_____

_____

_____

_____

_____

_____

_____

_____

_____

_____

_____

_____

_____

_____

_____

_____

_____

_____

## Final Thoughts …

_____

_____

_____

_____

## Feasts this Week

| | |
|---|---|
| **November 21** | **The Presentation of the Blessed Virgin Mary** |
| **November 22** | **St Cecilia** |
| **November 23** | **St Clement I** |
| | **St Columban** |
| | **Bl Miguel Agustín Pro (USA)** |
| | **Thanksgiving Day (USA)** |
| **November 24** | **St Andrew Dũng-Lạc & Companions** |
| **November 25** | **St Catherine of Alexandria** |

# Christ the King

THE RULE BY kings is not popular today. People living in democratic societies tend to be suspicious of kings and kingdoms. Citizens of representative governments prefer consensus and dialogue. The idea of one-person rule is too close to the experience of dictators. Jesus opposes the human kingship and powers of oppression and violence.

What, then, is this feast of Christ the King about?

The Scripture readings portray a different kind of authority. The prophet Ezekiel speaks of God as a shepherd who guides the scattered sheep with tender care. One might rewrite the image to say that the shepherd also leaves the one sheep and searches for the ninety-nine!

Paul uses strong language to evoke Christ's coming as one that abolishes "every ruler and every authority and power." The gospel portrays Jesus as Ruler of the End-Time. Like a shepherd he separates the sheep from the goats. "Just as you did not do it to one of the least of these..." This is indeed a new mandate.

Christ appears as the divine governor of the City of God. As citizens of "the City," Christians are called to challenge the many forms of violence in the world today with the charter of the Beatitudes, service, and self-giving love, especially to the needy and marginalized in society. May today's Eucharist give us the strength to do our part in building the City of God.

*Rev. Robert Dueweke, OSA*

**People and Prayers to Remember this Week**

_____

_____

_____

*Readings of the Day* —————————————————————

Ezekiel 34.11-12, 15-17                 1 Corinthians 15.20-26, 28
Psalm 23                                Matthew 25.31-46

**Responding to the Word**

**Jesus tells us that he will be present in others so that when
we do good to them we do it to him. What acts of kindness
and service to others can I do today to remind myself that
Christ dwells in them?**

_____

_____

_____

_____

_____

_____

_____

_____

_____

_____

_____

_____

_____

_____

_____

_____

_____

_____

_____

_____

_____

_____

_____

_____

**Final Thoughts ...**

_____

_____

_____

_____

**Feasts this Week**

**November 30    St Andrew**